The Mustard Seed
CHRONICLES

The Mustard Seed CHRONICLES

How God Equipped Women of Faith
in Home Group Meetings Through
the Power of the Holy Spirit

ANNE M. COCHRAN

GGP
GLORY GIRL PUBLISHING

GGP

Glory Girl Publishing
P.O. Box 11297
Charlotte, NC 28220
www.GloryGirlPublishing.com
Anne@GloryGirlPublishing.com

Cover image, "Mustard profiled against the California sky,"
used with permission from Shutterstock.com © Ken Kistler

Book and cover design by Angela Harwood

ISBN: 978-0-578-08935-5

"The Kingdom of heaven is like a mustard seed, which a man took and planted in his field. Though it is the smallest of all your seeds, yet when it grows, it is the largest of garden plants and becomes a tree, so that the birds of the air come and perch in its branches."

Matthew 13:31-32

THIS BOOK IS WRITTEN FOR and dedicated to God the Father, His Son Jesus, and the Holy Spirit who have loved me to the place where I can begin to be all it is I have been created to be.

AND TO ALL THE GLORY Girls. You have made this great adventure the ride of a lifetime, and I would not want to be on it with anyone other than you. You know who you are, and I love you.

CONTENTS

God does not call the equipped; He equips the called.

ACKNOWLEDGMENTS

FIRST AND FOREMOST, I WANT to acknowledge the Holy Spirit, who gave me the confidence to know that all things are possible for those who believe.

A big THANK YOU to:

Bill and Carol Grier, for having the vision and seeing it through.

John Peters, who was used by God in transforming my life through the baptism of the Holy Spirit.

Phil Tierney, who believed and came along beside me encouraging me to fly.

Alan Smith, who took the Glory Girls under his wing and graciously fathered us.

Betsy Thorpe, who edited this book and stretched me further than I expected; her encouragement, her talent and her belief in this book helped make it happen.

Angela Harwood who designed the cover and to Carin Siegfried, who came along as the copy editor to help with the editing details.

To all the guests the Glory Girls hosted over the years in my home. Your mentoring grew us up, and helped equip us so that we could become mature women of God.

To all the ministries, far and wide, that blessed us with your God-given talents. You provided valuable tools through your teachings, books, tapes, CDs, email devotions and conferences. Without you, we would not have been introduced to the things of the Spirit and started living life to the fullest.

To all the women who came through the front door of my home to meet together in order to know the Lord more intimately. Each of you has been an inspiration and a blessing in my life.

A special thank you to Esther Grant, Connie May, Nancy Moore, and Libby Walker who were willing to share their testimonies for the book.

And to my precious family: my husband Rob, who has given me the freedom to grow, and to my daughter Hallie and my son Rob Jr. Your support and unconditional love means more than you can ever know. I love you so very much, and pray the Lord will be ever-present in your lives always.

To Him be all Honor and Glory. Amen.

INTRODUCTION

THE MUSTARD SEED CHRONICLES IS the story of how a woman of faith chose to "trust in the Lord with all [her] heart and lean not on [her] own understanding but in all [her] ways acknowledge Him." (Prov. 3:5-6) It tells how the Lord initially met with me, and then taught, trained, and equipped a group of women, who became known as "the Glory Girls." It is a witness to God's ability to grow something for His Kingdom's purposes even though it may begin as something that looks as small as a mustard seed.

Matthew 13:31-32 says: "the Kingdom of heaven is like a mustard seed, which a man took and planted in his field. Though it is the smallest of all your seeds, yet when it grows, it is the largest of garden plants and becomes a tree, so that the birds of the air come and perch in its branches." I have come to see mustard seeds as more than just tiny seeds. I see them as opportunities the Lord gives us to grow deeper in knowledge of Him. When we grab hold of the opportunities the Lord gives us to deepen our relationship with Him, we are in essence holding out our hand and accepting a mustard seed He is giving us to plant. Once planted, it is up to the Lord to make it grow. He calls us to be good overseers of the little seeds. We need to pay attention to them, nurture them, and water them. However, God alone is the One who will make them grow.

When the word was first prophesied over me in 2003 that I would write a book, I must admit I just laughed. But I did receive the word. I wrote it in my journal and I believed. I accepted the seed. As the years went on, I would from time to time think about that seed. I held onto it, but never quite felt it was the right time to plant it. Then I had lunch with some girlfriends in August of 2010, and they asked me when was I going to begin writing my book. When I realized it was the week of my tenth anniversary of being baptized in the Spirit, I took notice. I went home, sat down, and prayed: "Lord, if it is time to plant this mustard seed, I am ready." And then I began to write. Time will tell how the Lord will make it grow.

I believe the Lord is calling me to share this story with you to encourage you to open your eyes and look for the mustard seed opportunities He wants to give to you today so you can not only get to know Him better, but also be part of His plan to further His kingdom here on earth. What I most hope to convey in sharing my story is this: when we say "Yes" to the Lord, a great and wonderful adventure with Him begins. And in the process of the adventure, we have the opportunity to watch His majestic power unfold before us as we see Him grow those little seeds into kingdom treasures. When we invite Jesus into our hearts and allow the Holy Spirit to be fully released in us, we begin to do His bidding here on earth to advance His kingdom, and those little seeds He gives us along the way will begin to reflect a part of who He is, all to His glory.

I believe there is no greater form of worship than to open ourselves up completely to the Lord, receiving all that He has for us to receive. I pray that *The Mustard Seed Chronicles* will open your heart of understanding so that you will not only see what mustard seeds can look like, but that you will respond to God's call in your life to do some planting. I pray this story will give you the confidence you may need to believe who it is God says you are, and as you hold out your hand to receive the seeds He has for you, I pray your "Yes" to Him will catapult you into your destiny call.

We serve a gracious, mighty, holy, fun, life-giving, purpose driven God. Open your hands. Accept the seeds. Start planting. I promise, you won't regret it. And I guarantee you will be forever changed because of it.

Anne
May 2011

CHAPTER 1

Let the Great Adventure Begin

"COME TO THE FREE LIVING and drink of it as often as you like." These are the very first words I ever heard the Lord speak to me. It was 4:20 A.M. on August 30, 2000. I was in my guest bedroom, unable to sleep and pondering all that had happened earlier that evening. I was also trying not to wake my husband Rob with my excitement.

I had attended a function at a nearby church to hear a preacher named John Peters, who was in town visiting from St. Paul's Anglican Fellowship in London, England. He had been invited to speak by the Evangelism Commission of my church. Reverend Peters was to talk for several days about Christian faith issues: the identity of Jesus, the centrality of the cross to Christian claims, the truth of the resurrection, and the Holy Spirit.

I had met John when he first visited our church back in 1994. He had spent several days as an invited speaker, talking about Questions of Faith. On the last night, John invited people to come forward for prayer, offering to pray individually with anyone who had a prayer need. I decided to go forward for prayer, not really knowing what to ask for. It was the first time I had experienced the laying on of hands other than when I was baptized as a baby and confirmed as a teen. It was the first time in a church setting that I had encountered anyone who offered to pray for individual needs in this way. As John began to pray for me, he prayed that the Holy Spirit would come into my life and that Jesus would come and work in my life. It was a simple and short prayer. He then laid his hand on my head, prayed a blessing over me, and that was it.

I remember going home and telling Rob about the prayer encounter and though I could not explain it, I felt something had begun stirring inside of me that I had no understanding of or frame of reference for. I found myself thinking about what the Christian life was suppose to look like and told Rob I felt I was trying to squeeze myself into a Christian mold that really did not exist. This is what I wrote in my journal: "It dawns on me tonight that all of us, though made in God's image, are unique in ourselves. We have our own special walk, talk, and our own special way of doing things. I pray the Lord will reveal to me what kind of Christian He wants me to be."

For the next several nights, I was teary but did not know why. I could not make sense of my emotions and had no idea where they were coming from. I knew it was somehow related to the prayer I had received from John. After a week or so, the busyness of life took over again. I did not give any more thought to John's prayer, my conversation with Rob or any of the emotions I had experienced. But when I heard John was coming back to town all those years later, that encounter from 1994 resurfaced. I was curious to go hear him teach again and made plans to attend the summer series.

After the first couple of nights of lectures, the fellowship of prayer group at our church asked John if he would add a night to his schedule and talk about prayer. Because this talk was not originally scheduled, it ended up that there was no place at our church to have the meeting. Eventually, someone found a church down the road that had space and was available to host the meeting. I called a couple of women I was just getting to know and invited them to go with me. I headed out on that Tuesday night not expecting more than to hear a good word and enjoy an evening with new friends.

John spent a good part of the night talking about how prayer is the language we use in our relationship with the Lord. "Prayer is not a ritual," he said. "It is relationship, and prayer draws us closer to God. Christians claim prayer is the most potent force of change in the universe. It is the love language to our Father, Abba, Daddy. He is our loving Father, and He desires an intimate relationship with us."

John went on to explain that the power of prayer depends almost entirely upon one's understanding of Whom it is we are speaking to. It is through Jesus that we have direct contact with the Father. "I am the way and the truth and the life. No one comes to the Father except through me." (John 14:6) And it is in the name of Jesus that we pray. "I tell you the truth, my Father will give you whatever you ask in my name. Until now you have not asked for anything in my name. Ask and you will receive, and your joy will be complete." (John 16:23-24)

Matthew 7:7 says: "Ask and it will be given to you; seek and you will find; knock and the door will be opened to you. For everyone who asks receives; he who seeks finds; and to him who knocks, the door will be opened." John said the most important thing to know about prayer is to keep doing it. Keep knocking! When we pray persistently, it shows we are in relationship with God. We need to believe that God does hear us and will answer our prayers, though not always perhaps in the way we would hope or desire. And then he said something very important: "It is prayer with the leading of the Holy Spirit that is key. Prayer is something we do in the Spirit of God with the help of the Spirit. The Holy Spirit is the One who teaches us how to pray."

John ended the evening, inviting us to stand and pray together.

He suggested we hold out our hands as if receiving a gift, and then he began to pray a very simple prayer, "Holy Spirit, come." This was not the norm in my church. I think it is safe to say that most of the folks who were there that night had not prayed together like this. No sooner had John prayed this simple prayer than something began to stir in my spirit. I don't know how to describe it other than it felt like I had butterflies in my stomach. John continued to invite the Holy Spirit to come. And then, John began to pray in tongues. It was the first time I had ever heard anyone pray in tongues. Suddenly, my ears tuned in to this new supernatural sound. I was fascinated. John began going around the room encouraging others in the room to pray out loud, either in English or in tongues. I was surprised to find that several other people began praying in tongues and I remember standing there, trying to hold back a flood of emotions that were welling up. I don't remember too much after that, other than eventually John closed the meeting and everyone began to leave. Several of us, however, were left frozen in our places. Most of us were crying. "What in the world is going on?" I wondered. "Something is happening here and it is real and we all are being affected by it."

John came over to check on us and asked what was going on. "I don't know," I mumbled between tears, "You tell us!"

He explained, "You are being touched by the Holy Spirit." He then asked if he could lay hands on us individually and pray for the Holy Spirit to be fully released in our lives. "When they arrived, they prayed for them that they might receive the Holy Spirit, because the Holy Spirit had not yet come upon any of them; they had simply been baptized into the name of the Lord Jesus. Then Peter and John placed their hands on them, and they received the Holy Spirit." (Acts 8:15-17) Everyone agreed, and John began praying individually over each one of us.

When my turn came to receive prayer, it was like nothing I had ever experienced. As John laid his hand on my head and prayed for the Holy Spirit to come, it was as though electricity began to run through my entire body. I was so overcome with the physical presence of God that my emotions gave way and I wept and wept. For the next hour or so, we sat together in the midst of the raw emotion we were experiencing. God's presence permeated the room. It was wild. It was crazy. It was scary. It was supernatural. And it was real. What an amazing night: a life-changing occurrence had taken place. I knew I would never be the same again. I had just received a touch from the King.

You can imagine how hard it was to get out of that church building that night. I don't think any of us wanted to go home. But eventually we had to leave and head our separate ways. I got in my car and sat there for a while. How do you reenter the reality of your life after you have had an encounter with God? I felt numb and things around me seemed surreal. My only thought was: "*Now* what am I supposed to do?"

When I got home, I was tired and emotionally drained, but at the same time excited and awed. It was late and everyone in my family was in bed, asleep. I tried to go to sleep, but couldn't. I kept wondering if what I had experienced was real. I tossed and turned for what seemed like the longest time and eventually I got up and went into our guest bedroom to sit and ponder and pray about all that had gone on.

It was then that I heard those words, not audibly in the room, but in my mind's voice. I knew they were not my own. It was the Lord: "Come to the free living and drink of it as often as you like." God, the Creator of the universe, the Father of Jesus, was speaking to me, a forty-two-year-old wife and mother of two, sitting alone in her guest bedroom. I knew this was an invitation, an invitation to enter into a new, deeper, and more fulfilling relationship with the Lord. That is really all I could comprehend at the time as I thought about those words. I knew in my spirit, my heart, and my soul that something had shifted, something had changed, and I was more than willing to receive all that those words could possibly mean.

You see, even though my parents had me baptized as an infant in the church, and even though I had gone through the motions of confirmation as a teen, I did not have an on-going personal relation-ship with God the Father, Jesus Christ, or the Holy Spirit. It wasn't until I was attending Bible study at age thirty-one that I truly ac-knowledged Jesus my personal Savior. It wasn't until I was thirty-one that I was truly saved and could truly call myself a Christian.

I had been attending years of Bible Study, I was going to church regularly, and was involved in doing "all the right things" in the church. Yet after all this time, things were suddenly looking very different to me. It was like a light bulb had been turned on! All those years, having accepted Jesus into my heart, seeking Him in Bible studies, I always sensed something was missing—I always felt there was more. There had been a woman named Carla, who year after year, kept getting put in my Bible study small group. And year after year, I was constantly surprised at her answers to the questions in our study. I knew she and I were reading the same verses week after week, but she was seeing things I wasn't. How was she getting the answers she was getting? Though her answers were making sense, I couldn't for the life of me figure out how she came up with what she came up with to share.

Now I knew the answer. I had been missing the revelation *only* the Holy Spirit can give. I had been reading the words, but not having the revelation behind the words. I was saved and had accepted Jesus in my heart and was promised eternal life, but now I was seeing that was not all of it! That was only *one part* of a *two-part* equation. There was a second baptism, the baptism of the Holy Spirit, and suddenly I found Scripture after Scripture to verify this truth. I don't know how I had missed it in all my years of Bible study but there it was, plain as day. It was like the scales fell off my eyes, and I could now see new truths in the Word that had been there all along. "While Apollos was at Corinth, Paul took the road through the interior and arrived at Ephesus. There he found some disciples and asked them, 'Did you receive the Holy Spirit when you believed?' They answered, 'No, we have not even heard that there is a Holy Spirit.' So Paul asked, 'Then what baptism did you receive?' 'John's baptism,' they replied. Paul said, 'John's baptism was a baptism of repentance. He told the people to believe in the one coming after him, that is, in Jesus.' On hearing this, they were baptized into the name of the Lord Jesus. When Paul placed his hands on them, the Holy Spirit came on them, and they spoke in tongues and prophesied." (Acts 19:1-6)

Jesus gives us eternal life and the Holy Spirit gives us access to the anointing, the power, and the unction that Jesus walked in. Scripture tells us that Jesus said He was going away so He could send the Counselor, the Holy Spirit, *to us* so that we could do greater things than He did. "But I tell you the truth: It is for your good that I am going away. Unless I go away, the Counselor will not come to you; but if I go, I will send him to you. But when he, the Spirit of truth, comes, he will guide you into all truth." (John 16:7,13)

Now I had been filled with the Spirit of truth, and I could not even imagine how that truth would affect my life from here on out. I soon learned that I had entered into a newfound understanding of forgiveness, peace, wholeness, and love that is so real and pure and available to everyone who asks, it was almost too much to receive. And just like Jesus, the Holy Spirit had been there all along just waiting for me to surrender to Him. A door opened for me that night, a door right to the Throne Room of God. "Come to the free living and drink of it as often as you like" were words that I did not fully understand that night, but I knew they were from the Lord. Were these words even Scriptural? I would later find out that they were.

In Revelation 22, the NIV titles the chapter "The River of Life." Listen to what verse 17 says: "The Spirit and the bride say, 'Come!' And let him who hears say, 'Come!' Whoever is thirsty, let him come; and whoever wishes, *let him take the free gift of the water of life.*" (Emphasis added.) I did not see this Scripture until almost a year after I heard the Lord initially speak to me. The treasure of those words was there all along waiting to be discovered. You can image my surprise, delight, and awe when I first saw them. The Lord always confirms His word. That night in August was the beginning of a ride that continues to this day to be one of surprise and wonder. I am so thankful not to be missing out on *the* greatest adventure of my lifetime.

Reflection

Do you know God the Father? Do you know Jesus? Do you know the Holy Spirit? Are you in relationship with the Father and Jesus, but have not made a decision to embrace the Holy Spirit? Maybe you at one time have been in relationship with the Father and Jesus and the Holy Spirit, but now realize you have not been actively pursuing them? Well today, you can change all of that. Today, you can begin or you can begin again. If you are ready to begin a personal relationship with Jesus, if you are ready to renew your relationship with Him or if you want to go deeper into your relationship with Him, then pray this prayer and invite the Lord Jesus into your heart. He is the best friend you can ever have. He is the kind of "friend who sticks closer than a brother." (Prov. 18:24) And He is waiting for you to take the step. Come on. How about committing today?

Prayer

Heavenly Father, I come before You today to tell You I want You in my life. Jesus, I believe You are God's son, who died on the cross for my sins. Through You Jesus, I have eternal life. Jesus, please come live in my heart.

I confess to You today that I have sin in my life, some known and some unknown. I am sorry. Today, on _____, I ask You Jesus, to please forgive me so I can begin anew. Thank You Lord for forgiving me. The Word says the blood You shed on the cross cleanses me and makes whiter than snow. Send Your Holy Spirit now so that I can be made into the person You created me to be. Come Holy Spirit. From this day forward, I ask You to lead, guide and direct me so that I may walk in my destiny. Thank You Lord. In Jesus' Name I pray. Amen.

Suggested Bible Readings

Romans 5:6-11; Romans 10:9-13; Galatians 2:20; Acts of the Apostles 2:38-41

A good resource to learn more about prayer: *Conversation With God: Experiencing the Life-Changing Impact of Personal Prayer,* by Lloyd John Ogilvie

CHAPTER 2

Double Blessing

THOSE FIRST WEEKS AFTER MY encounter with the Holy Spirit were rocky. I don't think it is an understatement to say I was acting a bit strange. I was getting up at 5:00 A.M. to pray, which was completely opposite from my normal routine. Before, I had been a three-time hitter of the snooze button. Now I was popping out of bed before the alarm went off so I could go into the guest room to pray. Rob took notice. I was crying a lot (I have since learned that I was going through a cleansing time) and all I wanted to talk about was the Holy Spirit and Jesus. The only people I really wanted to talk to were folks who wanted to talk about the Holy Spirit and Jesus. You get the picture. Our once fairly calm household was being shaken in a major way because of me. OK, it was really being shaken by the Lord.

I was so changed, spiritually and emotionally, that my relationship with my husband Rob began to suffer. I think it is fair to say those first weeks were probably the most difficult weeks Rob and I have had in our married life. Suddenly, life as we (he) knew it was turned upside down. Actually, *I* seemed to be suddenly turned upside down!

As crazy as it sounds, it took us about four weeks to finally sit down and really talk. When we talked about what was going on, Rob shared his fears. He admitted that my behavior was scaring him, and he was beginning to wonder if maybe I was going to leave him and head to Africa to go into the mission field. I was able to clearly tell him that night that no, I was not heading to Africa. I did not believe God brought us together in marriage for Him to then make Himself known to me so deeply in order for us to separate. And yet, as determined as I was to make that point, I was just as determined to make it very clear that I was never going to be the same again and I was never going back to the way I had been.

Neither he nor I had a clue what that really meant or what that would really look like, but we were able to reach a new place of peace that day and began to move forward in this new way of life. I bet Rob thought nothing would change much for him, and I bet he might have even thought I would eventually go back to my old ways again. That didn't happen. And little did we know what was coming. God's funny like that. I have learned He loves surprises and He sure did have one in store for the both of us. This transforming occurrence had a huge impact on me, but Rob was going to be touched by the wave of it as well and it was going to happen much sooner than either of us would have been able to anticipate.

The Butterflies

After that night of August 30, 2000, a group of six women (which eventually grew to eight) began meeting weekly on Friday mornings at my friend Anne Neilson's house. The purpose of these meetings was to come together and be with one another to talk and share about what was happening as a result of the teachings we had heard and the prayers we had received during John Peter's visit. We each had had a life-altering encounter with God and we found it was not something we could talk about with just anyone.

Those Friday mornings became a most sacred and intimate time as we fully committed to meeting each week. We gathered and invited the Holy Spirit to come, and found ourselves immersed in times of confession and repentance, in times of prayer and deliverance. We were able to get real with one another very quickly, and found ourselves sharing very personal things. It was really quite remarkable. But that's what happens when you get connected with someone in the Spirit. There is a supernatural trust that comes. 2 Corinthians 3:17 says: "Now the Lord is the Spirit, and where the Spirit of the Lord is, there is freedom." We began to experience new freedom in being ourselves. We called ourselves the Butterflies. God was pushing each of us out of our comfortable cocoons so that we could become the butterflies He had created us to be.

It was exhilarating as we experienced His presence in ways that were supernatural. I remember one time the literal Wind or Breath of God blew through the room as we worshipped Him. We all felt it and knew it was the Lord. There were other times the Lord's weighty presence encompassed us and we would sit quietly in reverent awe. Each week was different and each was special as we learned to surrender to the Holy Spirit and as we learned to hear His voice.

Worship music became very important to the Butterfly group as we embarked on this new adventure together. Psalms 42:7-8 says: "Deep calls to deep in the roar of your waterfalls; all your waves and breakers have swept over me. By day the Lord directs his love, at night his song is with me—a prayer to the God of my life." Worship is prayer, and it is a key component to entering into the presence of the Lord. "Ascribe to the Lord the glory due his name. Bring an offering and come before him; worship the Lord in the spender of his holiness." (1 Chron. 16:29) The first worship CD I ever bought was during these first months in the Spirit and was by a woman named Sheila Walsh. It is called *Blue Waters*. Psalms 100:1-2 says, "Shout for joy to the Lord, all the earth. Worship the Lord with gladness; come before him with joyful songs." I have found that I am a worshipper at heart. Nothing makes me happier than being in the presence of the Lord worshipping Him through music and singing.

Another important tool was given to us these first months by Anne's mom, Joy Lamb. Joy had written a book titled, *The Sword of the Spirit; The Word of God*. This fabulous book compiles Scripture, co-ordinating it in different sections so that you can pray Scripture for anything from personal prayers for healing, to prayers for comfort, forgiveness, and prayers for salvation. Joy also has a section of prayers that can be prayed for the nations and the world. Anne gave each of us a copy of her mother's book, and we used it as we learned about prayer and intercession. Months later, we all ended up traveling to Florida to spend a weekend with Joy and some other women friends of hers who were mature in the things of the Spirit. The Lord was faithful to us in these early days. We were babies craving spiritual food and He provided the opportunities to learn and grow. "Like newborn babies, crave pure spiritual milk, so that by it you may grow up in your salvation, now that you have tasted that the Lord is good." (1 Pet. 2:2-3) Those first years in the Spirit when I got to spend time hanging out with the Butterflies, presented a rare and unique opportunity for each of us. I am so thankful that I was a part of that amazing time in the Lord with those wonderful women of God.

Salvation and the Gift of Tongues

On the home front, the dust was starting to settle. I was trying my best to be sensitive to Rob and the kids, all the while excited and passionate about how my relationship with the Lord was changing. My every moment alone was consumed with the Lord and I found I was in constant prayer and intercession. I was also desperate for one of the gifts of the Spirit. I wanted to receive the gift of tongues. "All of them were filled with the Holy Spirit and began to speak in other tongues as the Spirit enables them." (Acts 2:4)

From the moment I had heard John and others pray in tongues that first night in August, I had a desire to receive that gift of the Spirit. I actually wanted *everything* the Holy Spirit had to offer. There was an inner desire not to quench the Holy Spirit no matter how strange or odd or unexplainable the manifestation of the Spirit may look in me or to others. So with that resolve, I began daily asking for all the gifts of the Spirit, especially tongues. "Now about spiritual gifts, brothers, I do not want you to be ignorant. There are different kinds of gifts, but the same Spirit. There are different kinds of service, but the same Lord. There are different kinds of working, but the same God works all of them in all men. Now to each one the manifestation of the Spirit is given for the common good. To one there is given through the Spirit the message of wisdom, to another the message of knowledge by means of the same Spirit, to another faith by the same Spirit, to another gifts of healing by that one Spirit, to another miraculous powers, to another prophecy, to another distinguishing between spirits, to another speaking in different kinds of tongues, and to still another the interpretation of tongues. All these are the work of one and the same Spirit, and he gives them to each one, just as he determines." (1 Cor. 12: 1, 4-11)

I was still rising early each morning. I would head into the guest room and begin praising and praying. I soon began noticing that my tongue was doing some odd "exercises" if you will, and I began to think that maybe this gift was getting ready to be imparted to me. I was struggling with control and trying to make it happen. I so desired it and I kept asking for it. Remember Matthew 7:7? When we keep knocking, God hears our prayers and He is faithful to respond.

Fast forward to Sunday, October 1. The church was hosting a speaker for one of the Adult Sunday school classes. His name was Davis Kuykendall, and he was part of Search Ministries in Charlotte.

Rob and I decided to go hear Davis speak as we had heard of him through friends. When Sunday school class was over, I suggested to Rob that we go introduce ourselves to Davis. Rob agreed and we approached Davis to say hello. As we introduced ourselves, Davis looked Rob in the eye and said: "I know you. I have been praying for you." Well, if looks could kill, that would have been my last day on earth. I knew Rob thought I was up to something and that maybe I had enlisted Davis as a co-conspirator. "Remember, I'm just meeting Davis for the first time too," I said. Then Davis explained to Rob that one of his buddies, Chris Boone, had mentioned Rob to him years earlier and Davis had been faithfully praying for Rob's salvation ever since. I am not sure how it all happened, the Holy Spirit is supernatural after all, but the next thing I knew, Davis was giving Rob his business card and asking him to call so they could have lunch. We then walked off and headed home and not another word was spoken about it.

What was most interesting to me about this encounter was I was hearing for the first time that someone other than me was praying for Rob's salvation. I had actually been praying for eight years for Rob to accept Jesus into his heart. When I met Rob, he was like a lot of folks who are regulars at church. He was a lot like I had been. He was faithful to attend Sunday services and once we were married, he even got involved in other church activities. Eventually he was elected to serve on the church Vestry. He was a long-time volunteer in the community and was known to be a man of integrity. Rob was and still is honest and hardworking, an all-around great guy. However, when I met him, and when I married him, he did not have a personal relationship with Jesus. So all through our married life, my quiet and fervent prayer was for him to accept Jesus into his heart and be saved.

Friday October 6 will go down in the Cochran history books as one of those amazing God days. I woke at 5:00 A.M. and headed to the guest bedroom for prayer and praise time and was so excited in my spirit that I started praising faster than I could follow; I could not understand what I was saying. All of a sudden I realized what was happening. I was speaking in a language I did not understand. I was speaking in tongues! I had no idea what I was saying. I did not receive the interpretation of the words but to be honest, I did not care. I was so excited I could hardly stop speaking for fear it may go away. It didn't, of course, and I've got to tell you, it was awesome. God had answered my heart-felt prayer and imparted to me that day a truly extraordinary gift.

I have since learned that not everyone is on board or in agreement about tongues and its significance in the Body of Christ these days. Some folks just don't even like to acknowledge it, talk about it, or admit to it. What is even harder for me to understand is that some folks don't believe it is a gift to be used for today. Guess what? It *is* a gift for today. There are entire congregations all around the world that operate in the gifts of the Spirit, and that includes the gift of tongues. I can honestly say I do not think a day has gone by that I have not used it. It is *that* special to me. I would encourage anyone who is seeking to receive all God has for them to ask for this spiritual gift. There are many books that have been written to help explain the influential power that praying in tongues releases. *Experiencing The Spirit*, by Robert Heidler, and *The Gifts of the Spirit*, by Derek Prince are two good ones to begin with. It is a gift that should be earnestly sought after. "For anyone who speaks in a tongue does not speak to men but to God. Indeed, no one understands him; he utters mysteries with his spirit." (1 Cor. 14:2) The Amplified version says: "For one who speaks in an unknown tongue speaks not to men but to God, for no one understands *or* catches his meaning, because in the [Holy] Spirit he utters secret truths *and* hidden things [not obvious to the understanding]." Praying in tongues is the purest form of prayer and the enemy cannot understand it.

That Friday evening, when Rob came home from work, I could not believe it when he told me he had had lunch with Davis Kuykendall. Shocked, I asked how it went. "We had a good talk," he replied, and then, in the blink of an eye, he said, "and I have decided it is time to declare." With that one small, quick sentence, I knew what Rob was saying. My husband announced to me that evening that he had decided to invite Jesus into his life. Rob proceeded to pull out a salvation prayer that Davis had given him and with me present, he prayed a prayer and invited Jesus into his heart. In a matter of minutes, everything changed again. I was suddenly witnessing eight years of prayer being answered. My husband was now signed, sealed, and saved. It was almost too much for me to take in. I was completely overwhelmed. I had received the gift of tongues and Rob had received the gift of salvation. Talk about a supernatural, miraculous day!

I did not share with Rob that Friday night what had happened to me earlier that morning. I didn't think it was the right time or the right thing to do. This was his moment in time, his moment to celebrate, his date to chronicle and remember. He had surrendered his life to Jesus. That really is the most important thing of all. We experienced a double blessing that day and it was a new beginning for both of us. What a mighty God we serve. I was beginning to see that He is there just waiting to pour out His blessings on us. I learned a valuable lesson that day as well. If we simply wait, trusting, and persevere in our prayers, which are the desires of our heart, the Lord will answer. 1 Chronicles 5:20 says: "He answered their prayers, because they trusted in him." I was seeing first hand that God does hear our prayers and He will answer them in due season.

Reflection

Have you been praying for someone to invite Jesus into their life? Has your prayer seemed to go unanswered? I want to encourage you today to believe that your prayer has not gone unanswered. Your prayers have been heard. Why don't you take some time now to write down the names of those for whom you have been praying? Then pray for each of them by name and thank God that He has heard your prayer and that His answer will come in just the right time. His timing is perfect. If He has placed it on your heart to pray for these people, then you can know it is on His heart too. Lift them up again today and believe. And make sure to document the day the prayers are answered. It is part of the testimony to His faithfulness. And is it always wonderful looking back, remembering all the Lord has done.

Prayer

Jesus, thank You that You are now seated at the right hand of God the Father and You are interceding on behalf of all of those I have felt led to pray for over the years. Hear again today the prayers of your servant. I want to lift up to You now_____ (name each one who is on your heart), and I pray that each one will come to know You, the Risen Lord. I pray that each one would be saved, in Jesus' Name. Thank You that in just the right moment You will answer my prayers, and that each one will enter into new life. You Lord are faithful to hear and answer. Thank You Lord. I submit these people to You now, in Jesus' Name. Amen

Suggested Bible Readings

Daniel 9:17; Matthew 21:22; Psalm 54:2; John 15:16

To learn more about Robert Heidler and his ministry, go to www.gloryofzion.org.

To learn more about Derek Prince and his ministry, go to www.derekprince.org

CHAPTER 3

New Life in the Spirit

A LOT WAS GOING ON these first weeks in this new life in the Holy Spirit, and I immediately began looking for as much information as I could to help me learn and understand who the Holy Spirit is. Someone suggested I read a book written by Dennis and Rita Bennett in the '70s titled, *Nine O'Clock In The Morning*. It is the story of how an Episcopal minister named Dennis Bennett came into a relationship with the Holy Spirit. I read the book in just a few days. The surprising thing is I also found another book written by Dennis Bennett titled, *The Holy Spirit and You* sitting on my bookshelf. To this day, I have no idea when I bought it, how I learned about it, or how long it had been there; but God knew a time was coming when I would need to read it so I could begin to understand the ways of the Holy Spirit. He does go before us and prepare the way.

The Holy Spirit and You was a wonderful first book for me to read to help me understand what the baptism of the Holy Spirit is all about. There was reference in the book about the importance of prayer meetings, and even though that in essence was what we were doing at Anne's each week, I found myself beginning to wonder if the Lord might be calling me to get something like that started at church. Therefore, I decided to go to Phil Tierney, the Rector of the church, to ask for his direction and to share with him what was occurring in my life. It was during our first meeting that I learned Phil had also encountered God through the Holy Spirit. He was very receptive to my enthusiasm and very willing to give me his time.

I talked to Phil about my sudden desire to become more involved at church and he offered to help me discern what it was the Lord wanted me to do. We talked and prayed. He asked questions and I answered them. He then said he was going to suggest some things for me to get involved with and I was to give him a thumbs-up if I liked the idea and a thumbs-down if I didn't. When he suggested I should get involved in heading up a new Spirit-led prayer meeting at the church, well, all I can tell you is, "I got a witness," to use a popular charismatic term. We ended the meeting and began walking the grounds of the entire church property, prayerfully discerning where the meeting should take place. Once we decided on that, we came up with a time and day to meet. Then Phil promptly sent me to the parish administrator so I could get an article in the church newsletter and get the word out to the congregation. Three weeks later, on September 21, 2000, I was leading my first ever Spirit-led prayer meeting at church, meaning we would invite the Holy Spirit to come and lead us as we prayed for the church. Looking back on it now, I see that the Lord was giving me my first mustard seed, inviting me to accept it and plant it.

Matthew, Mark, and Luke all tell the parable of the mustard seed. The mustard seed is a very tiny seed, so tiny in fact it is hard to imagine that when planted anything big would grow out of it. But in the parable of the mustard seed, the small mustard seed grows into a large tree, and it provides shade and safe dwelling for the birds of the air that come to sit in it. "The kingdom of heaven is like a mustard seed, which a man took and planted in his field. Though it is the smallest of all your seeds, yet when it grows, it is the largest of garden plants and becomes a tree, so that the birds of the air come and perch in its branches." (Matt. 13:31-32)

In 1 Corinthians 3:6-7, Scripture tells us that when we are given seeds to plant, we are called to water them but God is the One who makes them grow. What I see now, ten years after this journey in the Spirit began, is that each time the Lord calls me to begin something new or invites me to step out in faith to move in a new direction, it is like He is handing me a new mustard seed to plant. It may look very tiny and even insignificant at the beginning, but I have learned if the seed is from God, it will grow. This prayer meeting at church began as a tiny mustard seed. Little did I know I would be watering and cultivating it for three years. This special time set apart for worship and fellowship became a safe place for believers who were newly baptized in the Holy Spirit to come and grow in their walk with the Holy Spirit. It was a wonderful time of learning, maturing, and growing in friendship with members of the church.

Ten people showed up that first week and each time we gathered, we began our meetings by inviting the Holy Spirit to come and lead us in our intercession. I only had the experience of a few weeks at Anne's and the teaching from John Peters on how to enter into God's presence by inviting the Holy Spirit to come; so, I began the meeting each week that way. We would hold out our hands as if receiving a gift and pray, "Holy Spirit, come." I was excited and a bit nervous. I was also convinced that I was not to have any kind of agenda for the meetings. This was the Holy Spirit's time. All I needed to do was get the word out and invite people to come. I learned very quickly that the Lord was perfectly capable of taking care of the rest.

There was such expectancy and excitement to meet together, that any fears fell to the wayside. We would sit in a circle and be still. I would open with a simple prayer, and then we would wait upon the

Lord. One by one, as people began to hear a word or a prayer they felt was from God, they would pray out loud. For forty-five minutes we would just pray, one after the other, as we felt led by the Holy Spirit. This was a new experience for all of us but we were not daunted by the fact that we were just babies. Once you have a powerful encounter with God, your desire to meet with Him and your desire to relationship with Him far outweighs the worry of what you do not know. As we continued to meet, we learned how to relate with one another and we learned how to hear God's voice. I am sure there were many times we prayed prayers from our own desires instead of listening to what the Holy Spirit was saying. We were in "Spirit Led Intercession 101" and had so much to learn, but we did begin to grow in our knowledge of Him and we were always blessed by our time together. It was a wonderful time of new discovery.

Journaling and Hearing God's Voice

If there is one thing I would suggest to a person new in the Holy Spirit, it would be to get a journal and begin to write. There is no greater way to learn to hear God's voice than through journaling. The Holy Spirit is a wonderful teacher and as you begin writing in a journal, you begin to learn to discern the Lord's voice versus your own voice and even the voice of the enemy. Yes, he has a voice too. Mark Virkler has written a great book titled, *Dialogue With God.* It was one of the first tools the Lord placed in my hand as I began to learn how to differentiate between the Lord's voice and the other voices that we hear.

As I began to learn to hear God's voice, conversations would begin to flow between me and the Lord and I would write them down in my journal. I would be in prayer, and suddenly, I would hear a word or sentence or Scripture, and I knew it was the Holy Spirit talking to me. I would then begin to write, and would be in awe when later on I would reread what I had written. These intimate words from the Lord to me were sometimes directives on how to move forward in this new walk in the Spirit. But many times, they were like love letters. Here is an example of what that looked like. This is a journal entry from 2001:

> I heard the Holy Spirit speak, "Acts 6:15," so I got my Bible and read Acts 6:15: "All who were sitting in the Sanhedrin looked intently at Stephen, and they saw that his face was like the face of an angel." Then the conversation began.
>
> The Lord: "Do you want your face to look like the face of an angel, Anne?"
>
> Me: "Yes Lord."
>
> The Lord: "What do you think that looks like?"
>
> Me: "Joy! A brightness. A glow. A big smile, in my eyes and on my lips. A peaceful, calm presence—gentle and truthful. A presence that resonates, a look that makes others notice and feel peace, love, acceptance, holiness, light, all those things."
>
> The Lord: "You can't make yourself look like that. You can't control it. It is a reflection of what is on the inside—how My love penetrates you on the inside. Your heart, your mind, your soul, your body—My love shining out will make your face look like that of an angel. Be calm. Rest in Me. Learn the Word. Read the Word. Keep praying. All these steps will draw you closer to Me. Our love will deepen as our relationship deepens. Your eyes will become My eyes. Your lips will become My lips. Your words will become My words. Your thoughts will become My thoughts. Your desires will become My desires, and then you will have My face. Then, your face will be like Stephen's, like that of an angel. Joy, love, peace, patience, kindness, goodness, gentleness, faithfulness, and self-control—these fruits shining outward appear as the face of an angel. So rest, relax, pray, read, and let go—let go—be still, knowing I am God. And may the words of My heart fill your heart, as will My fruits, My grace, My holy presence. In all things Anne, desire Me, and your face too will shine like Stephen's."

Journaling and listening to a word from the Lord is a gift beyond anything I can describe. The Creator of the universe is jealous for us, His children. All we have to do is open ourselves up to Him today and listen to what He has to say. His words are life.

Dreams

I began to have dreams—lots of dreams. Most of them early on were about my family. God speaks to His people through dreams. "For God does speak—now one way, now another—though man may not perceive it. In a dream, in a vision of the night, when deep sleep falls on men as they slumber in their beds, he may speak in their ears." (Job 33:14-16). Through dreams, the Lord can give you a word of caution, a word of hope, a word of expectancy, a directive to pray for someone, even a word of love.

Dreams are fun to have and fun to interpret, especially when you have friends you can share them with. I'll talk more about this later on. John Paul Jackson is very gifted in dream interpretation and he has several materials available to help someone learn how to understand and interpret their dreams. I also love Ira Milligan's book, *Understanding the Dreams You Dream.* These are just two of the many dream interpretation books I have as resources. Not all dreams are from the Lord. As you learn to discern and interpret dreams, you will begin to learn which dreams are from the Lord and which ones are not.

Almost always in the beginning, when I had dreams about family members, I would wake up and go into intercession as the Lord led. Sometimes I would pray for their salvation. Other times, I would be led to pray for issues in their lives that needed healing and restoration. I ended up finding a book by Patricia A. Smith titled, *From Generation to Generation: A Manual for Healing.* This book was another tool the Lord gave me for my Spiritual tool belt. It is a great resource that expanded my understanding of generational intercession, and opened my understanding to issues that we combat in our lives because of generational sins. It gave me clarity and language for the prayers I was praying for my family during this beginning season in the Spirit.

Visions

I began to experience visions. Most of them were in my mind's eye, but I have had one open eye vision. It happened at a church prayer meeting the beginning of 2001. It was a rainy day and we had decided to keep the lights off in the classroom where we met. We prayed for about forty-five minutes and then just enjoyed the quiet and the Lord's presence. My eyes had been shut as I sat in the stillness when suddenly I was prompted to open them up. It was then I saw a dome of light resting on Carol Grier's head and shoulders. Her head was bowed in prayer and she did not know I was looking at her. I shut my eyes again thinking I must be seeing things but when I opened them back up, I saw the dome of light still resting on her. I just stared at it for what seemed like forever and then I heard the Lord say "shekhinah." Well, I had never heard that word before and had no idea what it might mean.

When we finished, I approached Carol, who at the time I hardly knew, and told her what I had seen. She got so excited that when I got home, I began searching my Bible and concordance for Scripture confirmation. "Shekhinah" is a word that means the glory of the Lord and it is described several times in the Bible. "It is a word used interchangeably with the word God and it means His presence 'dwelt in' or 'rested upon' someone who merited His favor."[1] Scripture describes God's Shekinah glory in Exodus 13:21, 24:15-17 and in Luke 2:9 to name a few. I would love to have more open eye visions like that. I know many people who do see in the spirit realm that way. It simply is not one of those things that happens very often to me.

Intercession

The visions I was having in my mind's eye continued to increase, especially when I was in intercession. The desire to pray increased at a rapid pace. I now know I am called to be an intercessor. One interesting thing that kept happening was a repeated vision of silver and gold dust falling from heaven when I would pray or intercede for my family or for a person the Lord placed on my heart. I had no idea what it meant, but in my mind's eye, I had this constant vision of this "dust from heaven" being released and falling all around my family, my home, our property, or the person I was praying for. It was a curious thing, one I just kept documenting, believing it was God, but not understanding what it could represent. I eventually shared this with Rector Phil, and he said it was a picture of new life from above being showered over me and my family. I have since learned that it is also a sign of God's glory, and the Lord manifests Himself in the natural world as gold dust. More on that later as well.

There would also be times I would find myself in my car, at the grocery store, or just standing in front of my kitchen sink when suddenly my prayer language would take over and I would begin praying in tongues. Sometimes I have an image of who or what I am praying for, and other times I don't. Opening yourself up to the Holy Spirit allows Him to use you when intercession for someone or something is needed. Intercession is a gift the Holy Spirit will impart to some people. Their main goal is to pray for the needs of others. "We do not know what we ought to pray for, but the Spirit himself intercedes for us with groans that words cannot express." (Rom. 8:26)

It has never bothered me that I don't know what I am praying when I pray in tongues. I know it is the Spirit praying through me and know that it is the purest form of prayer with no agenda, control, or manipulation attached, so I am at complete peace. "The Spirit searches all things, even the deep things of God. We have not received the spirit of the world but the Spirit who is from God, that we may understand what God has freely given us. This is what we speak, not in words taught us by human wisdom but in words taught by the Spirit, expressing spiritual truths in spiritual words. The man without the Spirit does not accept the things that come from the Spirit of God, for they are foolishness to him, and he cannot understand them, because they are spiritually discerned." (1 Cor. 2:10, 12-14)

Life in the Spirit was exploding for me and for all the ones I was meeting with weekly at Anne's and at church. Most of us dove right in to learning all we could and felt so blessed to have one another as we began this new exploration. One thing I have learned about life in the Spirit: when you are committed to know the Holy Spirit, He will bring people and resources along your path so you can grow and mature and begin to be all it is you were created to be. We are spiritual beings first and foremost. Learning to live in the Spirit is key if you desire to walk in the fullness of the Lord.

Reflection

Although the Bible is the best resource we have, the Lord also loves using us, His people, to advance His Kingdom here on earth. Today, I want to challenge you to begin looking at Scripture and at other resources about the baptism of the Holy Spirit. Then, read a new book or two written by men and women who have encountered God through the Holy Spirit. Reading testimonies about the baptism of the Holy Spirit from others who have experienced Him can be powerful and life changing. This is a real part of our walk as Christians. It is time we *all* walked in the power of the Holy Spirit. It is what the Lord desires.

If you are a believer, and have not prayed for the release or the baptism of the Holy Spirit, but are ready to take your relationship a step further, invite the Holy Spirit to be released fully in your life today. Below is a prayer you can pray, on your own or with others.

Prayer

Heavenly Father, I come before You, wanting more of You in my life today. I am asking for the Holy Spirit to be fully released in my life. Come Holy Spirit, come. I welcome You and invite You to be part of my life. Holy Spirit, I ask that in this moment, You begin to awaken my senses to You so that I can begin a more intimate walk with You. Holy Spirit, I want everything that You have for me. I do not want to quench the Spirit. Please come now, and release all the Spiritual gifts I have been designed to operate in. I pray that no weapon of the enemy will be allowed to rob, steal, or destroy my destiny call, and I thank You Holy Spirit that today, I begin a deeper walk with the Lord because You have now been fully released in my life. I bless You, Holy Spirit, and thank You for hearing my prayer, in Jesus' Name. Amen.

Suggested Bible Readings

Acts 1:5; all of chapter 2; Acts 4:8, 31-34; 6:2-6; 7:51, 55; 8:15-17; 9:17, 31; 10:44-48; 11:15-16, 23; 13:3-4, 52; 19:1-12, and 20:22, 27-37

Note

Some of you who just prayed that prayer might have a physical or emotional response. Others, however, may not. *Both are acceptable and right.* For those who do experience some sort of physical or emotional response, here are a few possibilities: some of you may begin to cry or weep. Others may experience a deep sobbing. Some of you may begin speaking in different tongues. Some may feel a vibration or shaking or something that feels like electricity moving in or through your body. Some may feel heat in certain parts of your body—like your hands or feet or ears. Some of you may have a vision or visions. Some may actually hear the Lord speak—audibly or in your mind's voice. These are *just a few* of many manifestations of the Holy Spirit you may experience. *But if you did not have an immediate physical manifestation, don't worry.* Once you invite the Holy Spirit to be fully released in your life, He will begin to move in your life. Remember, "everyone who asks receives; he who seeks finds; and to him who knocks, the door will be opened." (Matt. 7:8) You *will* begin to see things in a new light.

Make a note of today's date. This is a very important date in your life as a Christian. And make sure you share this with someone who is already baptized in the Spirit. You can also go to my website, www.glorygirlpublishing.com and share your testimony. I would love to hear from you. Keep your eyes focused on the Lord, and let the great adventure begin!

_____ Date I received the baptism of the Holy Spirit.

Other Books

"*Miracle in Darien*" by Bob Slosser
"*Intercessory Prayer*" by Dutch Sheets
"*Growing in the Prophetic*" by Mike Bickle

CHAPTER 4

Inner Healing, Soaking Prayer, and the Gift of Prophecy

I FOUND MYSELF EMBARKING ON a more personal journey as I continued praying with others at Anne's and at church each week. Even though I was beginning to feel a new confidence and a sense of purpose growing in me, I also became aware of the need for some healing in my own heart and emotions because of past hurts and sins in my life. I began to seek men and women of faith who could help me with this sudden awareness, and I prayed that the Lord would bring just the right people into my life at just the right time. He was faithful to hear my heart's cry. He loves His children and cares for them so. "The righteous cry out, and the Lord hears them; he delivers them from all their troubles." (Psalm 34:17)

As I started sharing deep hurts, pains, and areas of past sin in my life with the prayer group at Anne's house, I began to see that I had not received forgiveness to the depth it was offered through Jesus and His sacrifice on the cross. "If we confess our sins, he is faithful and just and will forgive us our sins and purify us from all unrighteousness." (1 John 1:9) There were things from my past I had asked forgiveness for and had even believed they had been forgiven, but now I became aware that I had not fully forgiven myself. I had places of deep shame, guilt, and embarrassment, and I wanted to be set free. I was beginning to see that those feelings and emotions were keeping me from moving forward and being whole; they were keeping me from loving myself for who I was and they were keeping me from embracing all life had to offer. Thus began my quest for inner healing.

Inner Healing

Inner healing is a term used to describe healing *in* your soul. Your soul is your heart, your mind, your will, your personality, and your emotions. Psalm 103 is a well-known Psalm that talks about the forgiveness the Lord offers. Verse 12 says: "as far as the east is from the west, so far has he removed our transgressions from us." In Micah 7:18, we read: "Who is a God like you, who pardons sin and forgives the transgression of the remnant of his inheritance?" I have always believed the Word of God is true and have always accepted it for what it says. I knew in my head I was forgiven, because that is what Scripture says, but I was realizing I had not received that forgiveness in my heart.

Guilt, shame, and embarrassment are inner feelings that can really weigh a person down. They can keep you in a kind of bondage. That bondage can have an effect on the way you live your life. I was seeing with more clarity that my inner issues were still causing turmoil within me, and I wanted freedom. I knew that I was a new creation in Christ, and I wanted to be myself and accept myself for who I was now and who God created me to be. "Therefore, if anyone is in

Christ, he is a new creation; the old has gone, the new has come!" (2 Cor. 5:17) I was beginning to understand with more clarity what Jesus did on the cross for me and it was astonishing. "He himself bore our sins in his body on the tree, so that we might die to sins and live for righteousness; by his wounds you have been healed." (1 Pet. 2:24).

As a young child, a teen, and even into my early adulthood, I never had a real sense of self-worth. I didn't have much self-confidence while I was growing up, and I never felt very important or significant. I did not feel cherished or loved or really special. Low self-esteem and low self-worth took me down a road of looking for love and acceptance in all the wrong ways and in all the wrong places to quote an old song. I had no real sense of who I was or what I wanted to do in life; I had no real direction, no real hopes, and no real dreams. I was just living life, getting by the best I could. Our perception is our reality, and my perception of myself sent me down a path that eventually became destructive. In my late teens and twenties, I was partying a lot, trying to fit in, and making bad decisions, all the while feeling very lonely, sad, and worthless.

When I turned thirty, an opportunity to move to Charlotte for a new job presented itself to me. I jumped at the possibility to move to a new place as I saw it as a chance to start life again and do things differently. It's not that a move can change your past, but I had a real sense of hope for a new beginning, a chance to start over, and this job opportunity was just the thing to usher in new possibilities and a new chance at life. I moved the spring of 1989. No sooner did I arrive in Charlotte, than God's plan for me began to unfold. He has a plan for each of us. "For I know the plans I have for you,' declares the Lord, 'plans to prosper you and not to harm you, plans to give you hope and a future.'" (Jer. 29:11)

Within one year of moving to Charlotte, I had a new roommate. Lizzie Swayze was the first Christian friend I ever had. She and I moved into a two-bedroom apartment right across from two new neighbors who also happened to be Christians. I found out that Bible Study Fellowship (BSF) was meeting in the church right across the street from where we were living. Talk about a set-up! That fall, I began attending BSF. The study was on the book of John. Within three weeks, I came to the realization that Jesus was what I had been looking for all along. In three short weeks, I could clearly see for the first time that Jesus offered love, hope and acceptance, all the things I had been looking for for so long. I finally understood that He is the One who loves me just the way I am. He accepts me with no hidden agenda. He wants to be with me and spend time with me. It was crystal clear.

So at age thirty-one, I invited Jesus into my life and my life was forever changed. I remember the night I came home from Bible study and got on my knees by my bed. I had gotten what was called an Assurance Letter from the lead teacher at BSF, Ruth Snyder. It was a pamphlet that takes you through steps that would assure you that you were in fact saved; believing God is who Scripture says He is, admitting your sins, confessing those sins, and then believing that Jesus took care of those sins on the cross. I invited Jesus into my life, and by faith believed He was in my heart and my eternal life was secure. It was a powerful night and one that ushered in an immediate sense of acceptance and peace.

However, it was through the baptism of the Holy Spirit that I was transformed. A veil was removed from my eyes, my mind, and even my heart as the Holy Spirit was released in my life. The difference was tangible, and now I was able to see the inner places in my heart and emotions that were still hurting and desperately needed healing. I wanted to walk in wholeness and be all God created me to be.

Soaking Prayer

Through a set of what I term "God circumstances," I was fortunate to have the opportunity to meet two women who lived in Concord, North Carolina, which is just down the road from Charlotte. Their names were Deborah Monroe and Peggy Johnson. Deborah and

Peggy were part of a small Episcopal church in Concord that had an inner healing ministry team in place for their parishioners and anyone else who wanted to come see them for inner healing prayer. They were two of several other women involved in a prayer ministry there called soaking prayer.

Soaking prayer is when two or three prayer ministers meet with the person needing inner healing, and they invite the Holy Spirit to come minister to that person. It is usually a sweet, quiet, and precious time with the Lord. Not many words are spoken by the prayer ministers themselves during a soaking prayer session; however, they will speak if the Holy Spirit leads them to. The Holy Spirit is the One who does the ministering in His supernatural way, and it is a time that usually ushers in deep healing to wounds in the heart.

During one of my soaking prayer sessions, Deborah had a vision in the Spirit. At the end of the prayer session, she shared it with me. "Anne, in the vision, I saw you kneeling on the floor with your arms stretched out. It was a setting of humility and peace. A huge white dove, as big as a person, descended from above and was carrying a pouch. The dove laid the pouch on the ground beside you and opened it. Inside the pouch was a sword, a shield, and a vial of oil. The words I heard at first were confusing but then I was able to make out what was being said: 'Be patient. Preparation time. Be patient. The time will come. That which you are meant to have will be given to you.'"

Deborah had a prophetic vision and received a prophetic word for me. Prophecy is a gift of the Spirit and it is the foretelling or revelation of things to come. When it is from the Lord, it is life-giving to those who hear it and it is a valuable gift for the church today. "But everyone who prophesies speaks to men for their strengthening, encouragement and comfort. He who prophesies edifies the church." (1 Cor. 14:3, 4) I cannot tell you how much her words blessed me then and bless me even now as I write them.

I have referred back to that vision many times over the years as I interpret the prophecy like this: The sword is a war weapon, and in Scripture we learn God's Word is our war weapon. In Ephesians

6:17, God's Word is called the sword of the Spirit and in Hebrews 4:12 it says: "For the word of God is living and active. Sharper than any double-edged sword, it penetrates even to dividing soul and spirit, joints and marrow; it judges the thoughts and attitudes of the heart." A shield is another weapon of war that offers protection and in Scripture it is sometimes used to describe the Lord Himself. "But you are a shield around me, O Lord." (Ps. 3:3) A vial of oil first and foremost makes me think of anointing oil like the oil used to anoint priests. "Take the anointing oil and anoint him by pouring it on his head." (Exod. 29:7). Oil also represents healing. "Calling the twelve to him, he [Jesus] sent them out two by two and gave them authority over evil spirits. They went out and preached that people should repent. They drove out many demons and anointed many sick people with oil and healed them." (Mark 6:7, 12-13)

This was a powerful picture of promise. I saw this as a sign of what the Lord was equipping me with, and the words Deborah heard were just as important as the picture. I knew I was in a training time and I had to be patient, believing when the time was right, I would begin to walk in the revelation and the unction of the Holy Spirit according to His will so that I would one day be able to co-labor with Him to do His work here on earth effectively. "The Lord is faithful to all his promises and loving towards all he has made." (Ps. 145:13)

As a result of this vision, I began to research the gift of prophecy and tried to find out as much information as I could about this gift. 1 Corinthians 14:1 and 3 says: "Follow the way of love and eagerly desire spiritual gifts, especially the gift of prophecy. Everyone who prophesies speaks to men for their strengthening, encouragement and comfort." Jack Deere wrote a great book titled, *The Beginner's Guide to the Gift of Prophecy*. It is straightforward and easy to understand. I would recommend it as a wonderful resource for those interested in learning more about this gift of the Spirit.

MorningStar Publications and Ministries is a local ministry that operates in the prophetic. MorningStar is constantly offering opportunities to learn about life in the Holy Spirit through conferences, schools and teaching sessions. MorningStar is located on the Heritage property in Fort Mill, South Carolina.

There is also another ministry in Fort Mill called Chavda Ministries International. Doctors Mahesh and Bonnie Chavda are the Pastors of this church. During a conference weekend at Chavda Ministries International, I received my second prophetic word.

Gift of Prophecy

The conference weekend at Chavda Ministries International offered an opportunity for guests to receive prophecy. Carol Grier and I had become fast friends, and she and I attended the conference and decided to sign up to receive prophetic ministry. I met with three people, one man and two women. I had never seen them before, and they knew nothing about me or my encounter with the Holy Spirit. After they invited the Holy Spirit to come and release revelation, the man began by reading a Scripture to me from Deuteronomy 33:27 that says: "The eternal God is your refuge, and underneath are the everlasting arms. He will drive out your enemy before you saying, 'Destroy him!'" He said it was to be a life verse for me as I ventured out in my walk in the Spirit.

Then one of the women said, "Anne, I feel like this is a training time for you. A lot of conditioning is going on. Like all runners who run a race and have an extensive training program, I see the Lord massaging those muscles, getting you ready. You are like a horse about to be let out of the stall. So just relax in the time that you have. Let Him do His work and don't worry."

The second woman then said, "You have authority and I see you in the kitchen with a chef hat on and you are the head chef and you are telling people what to prepare and how things are to be done. They are in training on how to get things done." They ended with this: "All these words spoken are meant to encourage you that there is a calling on your life higher than what you've assigned yourself to or what others may have told you. So don't sell God short by looking too low."

Once again I received a word that confirmed my walk with the Lord and affirmed me as well. I *was* in training and it *was* a time of conditioning. And unbeknownst to me, I would soon be let out of the stall. I would soon be leaving the church prayer meetings and opening my front door to host meetings in my home. The kitchen would become one of the main gathering places as I served up real food and spiritual food to all the women who would come to my home. Prophecy is an amazing gift to share and to receive. We all would be wise to press in and learn to clearly hear God's voice through the Spirit so we can bless one another with encouraging, life-giving, and sustaining words that offer hope, inspiration, vision, and peace.

As my quest for inner healing got underway, those feelings of guilt, shame and embarrassment from past mistakes slowly began to disappear. To this day, I continue to seek prayer ministry as the Holy Spirit reveals places in my heart that still need healing. To me, this is what sanctification looks like. It's the on-going process of becoming whole, of being transformed more and more into the likeness of Jesus. Although I know I still have issues to work on, I have come a long way, and I trust the Lord to see me through as I continue to surrender more of myself to Him.

Reflection

Do you find that there are some things in your past that still cause you hurt, pain, shame, embarrassment? The Lord wants you to once and for all give them over to Him today. Get in a quiet place and invite the Holy Spirit to come. Ask the Holy Spirit to lead you in prayer today so you can lay at the foot of the cross the things that still cause you to feel bad about yourself. Jesus died on the cross so that we could be released from those past mistakes, those past sins, those past experiences. Go to Him now in prayer and receive His forgiveness. He is waiting for you. He is ready to set you free.

Prayer

Holy Spirit, I want to be set free from the guilt and shame, the embarrassment and pain that is with me because of _____ (speak out the issues to the Lord). Today I want to lay these things at Your feet at the foot of the Cross. I want the blood that You shed to wash over these feelings so that I can be made new. I want to receive Your forgiveness to the full extent in which it is offered to me. Your word says, when I confess my sin, You are faithful to forgive and cleanse me from all unrighteousness. (1 John 1:9). Lord, today I receive Your forgiveness as I let go of those things that have hindered me from moving forward to live my life according to Your will and Your ways. I decree that today, I am set free. I am free in Jesus' Name. Amen

Suggested Bible Readings

2 Samuel 22:1-7; Psalm 25; Psalm 130; 2 Corinthians 3:18 (NLT)

CHAPTER 5

Change Is Coming

GOD IS SO STRATEGIC IN the way He orchestrates things. The equipping and training I had been part of was going to be important for a new assignment He had in store for me. In September 2001, a second wave of the Holy Spirit's baptism happened at our church as John Peters was invited back again. It was the week of September 11, and the church was packed on Sunday following that horrific event. John invited the Holy Spirit to come during the church service and many more were baptized in the Spirit that day. As a result, more people started coming to the church prayer meetings, which meant an entirely new group was forming. We became a larger body of believers who had been deeply touched by the power of the Holy Spirit, and we continued to learn from one another and support one another and grow in the Spirit with one another.

We continued to meet every Thursday at church except Thanksgiving Day. I got to know some wonderful people during this season of my walk. We had a common bond. The Holy Spirit wove us together in friendship and our deep desire to seek the Lord above anything else was the glue that held us together. It was a time of learning, maturing, and a time of true discipleship.

Joni Ames

In February of 2003, our church prayer group hosted our first guest speaker, a woman named Joni Ames. I first heard of Joni through the Elijah List. The Elijah List is an on-line prophetic news source that Steve Shultz began back in the 1990s. He currently sends out daily prophetic articles from tried and true prophets all over the world to over 134,000 e-mail subscribers through the Elijah List. It has been a lifeline and valuable source of information to me and others in the prayer group as we have desired to learn all we can about the prophetic.

Joni was a featured writer for the Elijah List and when I saw she was from Charlotte, I decided to contact her. I sent her an email telling her about our church prayer meetings, and I invited her to visit and talk to us about the gift of prophecy. To my complete surprise she not only responded, but accepted my invitation. Ten days later, Joni was spending a Thursday morning with us.

Joni is head of ACTS Ministry (Activating Christians to Serve). She spent the morning talking to us about the importance of learning to hear the voice of God and the gift of prophecy. As I said earlier, prophecy is hearing God's voice and then speaking it out. "Above all, you must understand that no prophecy of Scripture came about by the prophet's own interpretation. For prophecy never had its origin in the will of man, but men spoke from God as they were carried along by the Holy Spirit." (2 Pet. 1:20-21) Joni talked about the blessings and the pitfalls of giving a prophetic word, and she encouraged us to continue to grow deeper in relationship with the Lord so we could really discern His voice and bless others with words He had for us to share with them. She went on to remind us that there are false prophecies given from time to time, and there are also false prophets. "But there were also false prophets among the people, just as there will be false teachers among you." (2 Pet. 2:1)

Scripture says: "I know in part." (1 Cor. 13:12). We do not always hear correctly or speak out correctly. We have to learn to test and discern the spirits. "Dear friends, do not believe every spirit, but test the spirits to see whether they are from God, because many false prophets have gone out into the world." (1 John 4:1)

Joni reassured us that it was not something we had to worry about. The Lord will always show us if we miss the mark by giving a wrong word. We also need to pay attention and see if we have peace about a word that is spoken over us. If there is no peace, Joni said, we should pray about the word, sit on it, ponder it, and not act on it unless we get confirmation that it is a word from the Lord. It was a great teaching and we all learned a lot.

When Joni wrapped up the meeting, she offered to prophesy over each of us individually. Many women there had never had an opportunity to have someone prophecy over them and everyone was excited to receive a word from the Lord.

As Joni began going around the room blessing each woman with a prophetic word, we marveled at the accuracy with which she spoke over each person. Remember, we all knew each other but Joni was just meeting us for the first time. When Joni prophesied over one woman, Jenny Newman, she said she was seeing musical notes over her head. Joni told Jenny that the Lord would use her to minister to other people with a song. Those of us who know Jenny, know well that music is a huge part of her life. Sure enough, music not only ministers to her personally, but as she ministers to others, it is not uncommon for Jenny to get lyrics from a song to bless the person she is ministering to.

When Joni prophesied over Carol Grier, who was and still is a Christian counselor, she told Carol that the Lord was showing her that she was taking care of everyone else but herself, and then Joni said, "I have one word for you: boundaries." Little did Carol know then that several weeks after this word was spoken, she would begin teaching workshops about the importance of boundaries, using a book by Henry Cloud and John Townsend titled *Boundaries.*

Joni's ministry provided powerful evidence to the truth of this gift as we saw the Holy Spirit give Joni precise words of encouragement for each woman that day. It was a clear demonstration that hearing God's voice was real and authentic and we all were blessed by our time with her. "My message and my preaching were not with wise and persuasive words, but with a demonstration of the Spirit's power, so that your faith might not rest on men's wisdom, but on God's power."(1 Cor. 2:4-5)

Joni was the first person who ever prophesied that I would write a book. I feel it is appropriate to share the word I received that day.

Personal Prophecy February 6, 2003:

I sense the Lord wants you to know that you are walking into a time of change again and I see the Lord has taken you and turned you upside down and a lot of change is falling out of your pocket onto the floor. You've asked Him for it. I see you standing and saying to Him something to the effect of, "I want your divine interruptions Lord. I want You to invade my life in every area and I want change"—and with that may come a lot more change than what you originally thought but He wants you to know that it's Him. I know in the natural you have a hunger and thirst for the things of the Spirit but I feel that by the Spirit the Lord is telling me that He is going to pour out to you more than you can possibly imagine. And I feel like I see a book coming in the time to come and I just want to encourage you to journal and note take because I feel like what He is about, even here in this church, is an explosion of His Spirit, a radical explosion of His Spirit. So Lord I bless her and the part

You have for her in this and I thank You Lord for a mantle of humility to continue to be upon her Lord and that you would protect her Lord in that way in Jesus' Name.

All of what she said is true and it speaks to who I am. I *do* want the Lord to invade every part of my life and I have asked Him to do that again and again these last ten years. He has poured out more than I could have ever hoped for. And I sit here today writing in faith that this book will be not only be written but published as well. I pray this book will be an offering to the Lord, a blessing to the Body, and a blessing that honors Him.

Reflection

Has anyone ever spoken a prophetic word over you that made you jump for joy and experience a sense of purpose for your life? Maybe someone has spoken a word over you that you did not realize was prophetic. Maybe the word of life came from a teacher, an aunt or uncle, a mentor, or a coach. Maybe it was spoken years ago but it's coming to the forefront of your mind as you read this. Think about it for a minute. If something is coming back to you, I want you to remember it again now.

If you have seen the word come to pass, take this moment to thank the Lord. If it has not happened, take a moment to remember it again. Decree the word you received into the atmosphere, and thank the Lord that in His time, it will happen.

I think about Abraham. God gave him a promise that his offspring would outnumber the stars in the sky. Abraham got to see some of that promise come to life. And yet, it is still coming to pass today. I cherish the prophetic words spoken over me. You should too. And if you have discounted them in any way, tell the Lord you are sorry and receive them again. Psalm 145:13 says: "The Lord is faithful to all his promises." You can rest assured, His word is true and does not return void.

Prayer

Heavenly Father, thank You for the prophetic words.

They are life, they encourage, and they build us up. Thank You Lord, that You desire all of us to operate in the prophetic. *And we can*, when we learn to hear Your voice. I pray today that the gift of prophecy would be released in my life. Holy Spirit, give me words to speak to others today to encourage them, to give them hope, to bless them, and to show them You love them. Tune my ears to Your voice, and give me the faith and the courage to step out in this gift of Yours. Thank You Lord. All glory and honor is Yours, in Jesus' Name. Amen.

Suggested Bible Readings

Joel 2:28-32; 1 Corinthians 14:39-40

CHAPTER 6

Moving On and Moving Out

LIFE WITHIN THE CHURCH BODY was experiencing some difficult times as a result of all that had happened with the Holy Spirit. In John 3:8, we read the Holy Spirit is like the wind, blowing wherever it wants. The Holy Spirit can really mess up a routine and can wreak some havoc as He shakes things up. In Acts 2:2, we get a picture of what it looks like when the Holy Spirit comes into a place: "Suddenly a sound like the blowing of a violent wind came from heaven and filled the whole house where they were sitting." A lot of times the shaking the Holy Spirit launches can cause fear and concern. We either have to be willing to accept the Spirit and move with the Spirit, or we risk falling back into old patterns and ways of doing things. I don't think the Holy Spirit can come into a place and not have some kind of powerful effect. But, when all was said and done, the church decided to go back to business as usual. As a result, many of the folks who had encountered the Holy Spirit in a transforming way eventually left the church to go elsewhere.

I too was sensing the need to move out and move on, though I did not know exactly what that was going to look like. Joni's word about change confirmed what I had been sensing in my spirit. I felt the Lord had something new in store for me, and I knew it involved ending my responsibility as coordinator of the prayer meetings at church. When thoughts of change come to my mind, it is time to put that testing of the spirits into practice. For me, this is what that looks like: I get still and quiet and I begin to pray. I ask the Lord for confirmation so I can be sure I am hearing Him correctly. I want to be obedient to follow Him wherever He tells me to go. I am learning when God has something new for me to venture into, it means He is ready to give me a new opportunity. He is ready to hand me a new mustard seed to plant.

After a time of prayer and discernment, I was convinced the Lord was ready for me to move onto something else, so I wrote a letter to the church prayer group in August 2003 letting them know I would be stepping down as the coordinator of the meetings. At that time, there were about sixteen people who met regularly to pray, most of whom were women. For the first time I had to let go of something that I held close and dear to my heart. It was the first time I was letting go of something that I felt God had actually birthed and grown through me. Letting go, I found out, is not as easy as writing a note to tell others, it is time to move on. But Scripture is clear. There are seasons for everything. "There is a time for everything, and a season for every activity under heaven." (Eccles.3:1) I did not question God and ask why. I simply wanted to make sure I was hearing correctly and obey. I have learned there will be many times when we won't know the reason why we need to change course and move into a new direction. He is Father God and He knows best. Our only responsibility is to be obedient to His call.

I had some immediate response to my decision and my letter, some good and some not so good. I was even accused of listening to the devil instead of to God. Some questioned my decision saying I was being divisive. It was very painful. And yet, I made it through. It appears that the Lord has designed me in such a way that when I know He is speaking to me clearly about what to do, I have the courage to move forward regardless of what others say or think. It has to be the healing power of the Holy Spirit in me because I always used to be so concerned about what others thought and was so interested in pleasing everyone regardless of what that might mean for me. This is one of the most amazing things about the Holy Spirit. He ushers in such wholeness and freedom if we allow Him to. I was surely on a road of restoration.

I used this painful event to build up more of my faith muscle, and found myself becoming more secure in who I was. When accusation comes, I tend to press in further still to make sure I am hearing correctly. Was this really God moving me out? After more prayer, after more devotional confirmation, and after more encouragement from folks the Lord brought along my way, I was totally convinced it was the Lord's will that I take the next step even though not everyone supported me and even though I had no clue what I would be doing next.

Moving out and moving on turned out to be an even bigger and more amazing opportunity than I could have ever hoped for or imagined. God had something wonderful in store for me to be part of. He did have another mustard seed for me to plant! I am so glad I was willing to take a leap of faith and move on. He was giving me a chance to see firsthand that all things are possible with God. Everything is for Him and His glory.

I consequently resigned from organizing the church prayer meeting the end of August and waited to see what was in store next. "May the God of peace, who through the blood of the eternal covenant brought back from the dead our Lord Jesus, that great Shepherd of the sheep, equip you with everything good for doing his will, and may he work in us what is pleasing to him, through Jesus Christ, to whom be glory for ever and ever. Amen." (Heb. 13:20-21)

Sharon Lampke, who became part of the church prayer group in 2001, continues to remind me that during this time of waiting and transition, a group of women from the church prayer group came to my home one morning and met for prayer: "I remember so clearly gathering at your house and praying, 'Dear Lord, here we are, a group of Spirit-filled women without Spirit-filled leaders or teachers. Please send us teachers, Lord.'" God heard our prayer. Never in our wildest imaginations could we have foreseen what God was getting ready to put together for us. He was going to do far more than we could have ever dreamed possible.

Soon after I resigned from my leadership role at church, an opportunity presented itself to me. I was invited to be part of an intercession team for an event in Charlotte featuring Bishop Henry Orombi from Uganda, and I accepted. In October, I ended up going to a woman's home to pray for the event and there, I met another group of women who were interceding for the event as well. That is where I met Donica Hudson. Donica was the leader of Jehovah-Shammah Ministries (JSM). The ministry consisted of several Spirit-filled women who were teachers, intercessors, and gifted in the prophetic. JSM had grown out of a home prayer meeting. The purpose of the ministry was to unite the body of Christ for revival through outreach, teaching, and media.

As we visited and got to know one another, Donica tossed out an interesting idea. Her ministry team had put together a seven-week teaching on prophecy and I knew a group of women who were hungry for learning as much as they could about life in the Holy Spirit. She wondered if maybe I would like to invite my friends into my home, and JSM would come in and teach the seven-week course on prophecy. It was an interesting proposal and I said I would think and pray about it. It must have been the Lord's plan because I could not get the idea out of my mind.

Bishop Henry Orombi came to Charlotte with several other

ministers from Uganda as guests of a local church to preach the salvation message of Jesus. It was a wonderful time of teaching and being in fellowship with other believers. I not only got to meet Bishop Henry, but was also able to get to know another precious man in the Lord, Paul Ssembiro, who accompanied the Bishop on his visit to Charlotte. As time went on, I eventually hosted Paul in my home and became his friend.

Epiphany–First Day of Meetings in My Home

In December, it was clear to me I was to open my home for seven weeks and invite JSM in to teach. Donica and I had agreed to partner together and we finalized arrangements for me to host my first ever prayer meeting in my home. I sent out an email to invite women I thought would be interested in coming. On Tuesday, January 6, 2004, I opened my doors for my first official home prayer meeting. Donica and her team arrived to teach about the gift of prophecy. Twenty women showed up to attend the meeting, and it was wonderful. We ended our time together by standing in a circle, holding hands and praying for our husbands. The new little mustard seed the Lord had given me got planted that day and there was no way I could have known how it was going to grow. But grow it did into one amazing, huge, beautiful, marvelous tree.

It took me a long time to "see" another important sign to all of this. I did not purposefully plan to host that first in home meeting on Epiphany. It just happened that way. But what a prophetic sign it was. Epiphany is a Christian festival observed on January 6 to commemorate the manifestation of Jesus to the Gentiles in the persons of the Magi. It means: "an appearance or manifestation of a Divine being, a sudden manifestation or perception of the essential nature or meaning of something."[2] It was a profound prophetic symbol. The Lord was planning to manifest Himself in ways that were new and transcendent. His ways are truly magnificent.

Reflection

Do you feel like you are supposed to move out and do something different? Are there new opportunities being presented to you that you think are of the Lord? Are you willing to do something new? Or are you comfortable in the way things are and don't want to change? I want to encourage you today to be willing to really look at the new opportunities being presented to you. Then ask a few people to come along beside you and pray about what you should do. It may be you are to stay put. But it may also be time for you to move out. Be willing to change. The Lord wants to use us to advance His kingdom. Lets be willing to be obedient to move in his direction.

Prayer

Lord, I want to let You know today that I am willing to move out and move into something new to advance Your kingdom if that is Your will for me. Holy Spirit, please show me clearly if I am to stay where I am, or if I am to venture out into something new. As new opportunities arise, give me clarity so that my yes will be yes, and my no will be no. Thank You Lord. My heart's desire is to be obedient to Your will. It's all about You. I trust You to show me where to go. I pray this in Jesus' Name. Amen.

Suggested Bible Readings

Ephesians 2:10; Colossians 3:23-24; 2 Thessalonians 1:11-12

CHAPTER 7

Trust in the Lord

EACH WEEK I PREPARED MY home for the Tuesday meetings. I began by praying over the house and playing worship music before the women arrived. I provided coffee and tea and something to eat. The night before, I would rearrange all the furniture in my den so we all could gather together in one room. It was effortless. There were no worries or stress.

On Tuesday mornings, all of the women would begin arriving at 9:00. We would have some time to visit, and then gather in my den. The JSM team would begin the morning with prayer. After a time of prayer, one of the women would launch into a teaching about the gift of prophecy. When the lesson plan was over, we would move into intercession. Donica and her team would end the morning by offering prayer ministry opportunities. It was an exciting time.

My family was on board with my hosting the meetings, and at the time, my children were in elementary school, so they were on the bus by 7:15 and not home until 2:00. I did all my correspondence via email and always encouraged people to bring friends. Surprisingly, as the weeks continued, and the word got out, two to four new women would show up each week. Those interested in deepening their faith came to experience worship, teaching, ministry, and fellowship. Women from all walks of life and all denominational backgrounds were coming. What we all understood very early on was my home provided a safe environment for women to be themselves in the Holy Spirit. There was a freedom for everyone to express their relationship with God in any way they wanted. There was freedom to raise hands in worship, and freedom to pray in the Spirit during intercession. There was freedom to receive inner healing prayer for hurts and wounds, and there was freedom to laugh out loud, cry, and rejoice.

Although the teachings provided some structure, the Holy Spirit had free reign to interrupt at any time. "Just as each of us has one body with many members, and these members do not all have the same function, so in Christ we who are many form one body, and each member belongs to all the others. We have different gifts, according to the grace given us." (Rom. 12:4-6) We celebrated the differences we all brought to the meeting. I met some wonderful women in the Lord these early days. What a gift to make new friendships in Jesus.

JSM also brought in guest speakers from time to time, which added a different dimension to the meetings. Even though JSM was teaching us from the Word about the gift of prophecy, our horizons were also being expanded by the gifts and teachings from others that came to visit us. We hosted a local worship leader and his wife who spent the morning leading us in a time of worship. We hosted an African American preacher from Detroit who had a passion to restore prayer in the public school system. We were introduced to a woman from Inspirational TV who was gifted in dream interpretation, and she spent the morning teaching on the relevance of dreams for today and how God uses dreams and visions to speak to His people. It was a phenomenal time, as everyone who came was so hungry to learn everything they could about the Holy Spirit. The enthusiasm and excitement at the meetings was evident, and the speakers who visited us were as excited to be with us as we were to have them. It was like a water spigot had been turned on and the water was constantly flowing. "Jesus stood and said in a loud voice, 'If anyone is thirsty, let him come to me and drink. Whoever believes in me, as the Scripture has said, streams of living water will flow from within him.' By this he meant the Spirit." (John 7:37-39)

Because I had no agenda but to open my home for the Lord's purposes, He blessed us week after week. One guest speaker called us a "birthing center," as it was clear God was birthing all of us into new life in Him. And it was true. Weekly, women who had never encountered the Holy Spirit were baptized in the Spirit. Many of them received the gift of tongues. Several had visions for the first time. Others received inner healing as they confessed hurts and pains, and then received prayers for forgiveness and healing. Many lives were changed and transformed. God was drawing us closer to Him as we sought Him with all our heart.

On the administrative side of things, I was learning about the responsibilities involved with hosting twenty to thirty women in my home each week. I am a fairly organized person and enjoy administrative work, but I began to get a little concerned about the time frame in which we were operating. Some days women were still in my home when my children got home from school at 2:00. As we were nearing the end of the seven-week course, the enthusiasm was high, and Donica approached me about hosting another four-week series her team had put together. It was titled "His Presence," and the lesson plan was to further our understanding of how much the Lord desires us to have an intimate relationship with Him. I don't know if I really prayed about it. The momentum was such that I just said: "Yes, let's continue." Everyone was in agreement and it just seemed like the right thing to do. I knew, however, I needed to address the time issue so we could be better facilitators and stewards of our time.

Instead of calling Donica to talk about my concerns, I sent her an email. That ended up being a mistake. Unbeknownst to me, the way my email was worded offended the JSM women and unfortunately, none of them called to let me know. It was not until the next week when they showed up at my house for the meeting that I found out. They sat me down before everyone else arrived to tell me how upset they were with me. It was a most unpleasant encounter, which ended with me being in disbelief at what was happening and in tears. By God's amazing grace, I managed to get it together for the meeting that day, and we did continue with the plans to move forward for the next four weeks. It took some time, but slowly over the next few weeks, this behind-the-scenes conflict resolved. I personally met with Donica to clear the air, and when the four-week session was up, and the meetings with JSM ended, we parted on friendly terms.

As I write about this now, I wonder what role the enemy may have had in the misunderstanding with JSM. He likes to get in the way and cause problems in hopes of derailing the things the Lord is doing. I guess I will never know. What I do know is that it was not my first experience with conflict, and most assuredly won't be my last; but with God's help, conflicts won't ever keep me from moving forward in the things He has for me to do. Conflict is not fun, but the Lord's purposes were being fulfilled in these meetings and that far outweighed anything that may have come along that was uncomfortable. As we grow and mature in the Spirit, there will be times of contention and testing, discerning, and correcting. There is a Scripture that says, "As iron sharpens iron, so one man sharpens another." (Prov. 27:17) This experience gave me a clearer understanding of what that meant and what it could look like.

We learn through encounters we have with people and through circumstances that come our way. Those experiences help mold and shape us. I was learning that I was ultimately responsible for what was going on in my home. I was learning how to oversee the activities and be proactive in setting boundaries. I was learning how to properly communicate. We all make mistakes. Sometimes, it will be the host who makes a mistake and sometimes, it will be the guests. It's just the way it is. None of us are perfect. What amazes me is God's faithfulness in the midst of conflict. "Lean not on your own understanding; in all your ways acknowledge him, and he will make your paths straight."(Prov. 3:5)

The more we mature, the more grace-filled and humble we will be in dealing with surprising conflicts. It is a sign of maturity when we can be forgiving and kind to one another, and loving in the midst of the turmoil. "Consider it pure joy, my brothers, whenever you face trials of many kinds, because you know that the testing of your faith develops perseverance. Perseverance must finish its work so that you may be mature and complete, not lacking anything. Blessed is the man who perseveres under trial, because when he has stood the test, he will receive the crown of life that God has promised to those who love him." (James 1:2-4,12)

As the summer approached and the meetings with JSM were wrapping up, the Holy Spirit kept reminding me of a woman I heard lead worship at a conference: Anjie Carpenter. She too lives in Charlotte. I sent an email to her to tell her about our meetings and asked if she would be willing to come spend a morning with us and lead us in worship. Anjie responded immediately and accepted my invitation. On April 4, 2004, Anjie came to our meeting and led worship for a while that day. Neither Anjie nor I could have known then that this was the first of many meetings to come. God's plans for these home meetings were just beginning to unfold. All we had to do was continue meeting. He was going to take care of the rest.

Reflection

Have you found yourself in an uncomfortable situation with a friend? Or maybe with someone you see at work or at school? Maybe even in your Bible study group? When there is trouble in our relationships, everyone can feel awkward. Whether you are the one at fault or not, times like these need humility and forgiveness. Sometimes we need to take the first step and be the one to break the ice. If you are in a relationship with someone, and something has happened to cause dissension, I want to encourage you today to be the one to extend the olive branch. If you don't do it, it may never happen. Be the one to take the first step to make amends. And forgive. Take the step of forgiveness today, even if you don't feel like it. Tell the Lord how you are feeling. Tell Him everything. (He knows it already.) And then, ask the Lord to help you take the right steps to mend the conflict. You will be a better person for it, and the benefits far outweigh the sorrow unforgiveness carries.

Prayer

Heavenly Father, I come to You today to ask for Your help. This current situation with _____ (name it out loud) is causing hurt, heartache, anger, and pain. I need You to help me forgive in this situation. Holy Spirit, I am asking You to lead, guide, and direct me in my next course of action. If I am to stay quiet for now, help me stay quiet. If I am to make a call and speak a word, please tell me what to say. Your Word says I have to forgive in order to receive forgiveness. I want to be in right standing with You, and I want to walk in Your ways. Help me today, I pray, and show me the way to go. I ask this in Jesus' Name. Amen.

Suggested Bible Readings

Ephesians 4:31-32; Colossians 3:12-14; 2 Corinthians 2:5-8; Matthew 6:14-15

CHAPTER 8

The Outpouring: Part 1

WHAT I THOUGHT WAS A seven-week commitment hosting meetings had now turned into a five-month gathering. Still, it felt like we were not done. Summer was upon us and school was getting out. There were twenty-five women who had an excitement and desire to continue to meet. I knew I had to keep my door open and I knew the meetings should continue. Anjie and I had connected with one another and she was interested in spending time with the group to teach us about worship. So after a couple of sporadic gatherings over the summer, our meetings picked up again in August 2004. Thus began a most incredible season with the Lord that we still talk about to this day. I refer to this time as "The Outpouring." God poured

Himself out to us in ways we could have never imagined. He brought people from all over the globe to teach us and minister to us. He fashioned every meeting in such a way that they built on one another. It was a supernatural time, and I continue to marvel at all that took place as I look back at all He did during this season in the life of our meetings.

Anjie Carpenter

I believe the Lord handpicked Anjie for this next season of our meetings. Anjie is a Spirit-filled woman of God, a wife, a mother of three, and a prophetic singer, songwriter, and worship leader. I asked her to share part of her testimony for the book, and this is what she said:

As a young girl of about seven, I began to ask my mother persistent questions that needed spiritual answers, questions such as, "Mommy, why is the sky blue?" My mother had given her heart to Christ as a child, but had been neglecting her faith and relationship with God as a married woman and young mother. She began to feel convicted that she should take me to church.

I loved church from the very beginning. I can still remember the very first time I attended Sunday school and what the lesson was about. By the age of eight, God was strongly drawing me into a relationship with Himself. In the Baptist church we attended, every service ended with a chance to give your heart to Christ. One night, I remember being overcome with emotion and an overwhelming sense of God's awesomeness and holiness. I knew I needed Jesus in my life. I went forward and was led in a simple prayer to turn away from my sin, accept the cleansing blood of Jesus through His death on the cross, and give my life to Jesus. My faith was simple and complete, and I felt overwhelmed with happiness and peace. I was baptized a few weeks later, which was an important moment for me as well. My Sunday school teachers encouraged me to read my Bible and pray every day, which I did. I grew quickly, and remember having the distinct feeling, when reading Scriptures, that God had written particular verses with me in mind.

As I grew in my faith, I began to be deeply burdened for my father. I remember once sitting on his lap and saying, 'Daddy, don't you want to go to heaven when you die? Don't you want to ask Jesus into your heart?' God used this to work on my dad. Within a year or so of my salvation, my dad agreed to go to church with us. He was eventually radically saved and went into full-time ministry.

Anjie was instrumental in expanding our horizons about life in the Spirit. She also helped us to trust one another as we got real with ourselves and began to function together as a group. One of the amazing things about being in the Spirit, as I have mentioned earlier, is the instant connection when you gather with people in the Spirit. And that is what had happened when Anjie first joined our group. Although she was initially with us to teach us about worship, she had much more to offer and we soaked up everything she had to share. She was a perfect fit for the group, a wonderful teacher and Spiritual mentor to all of us.

I'll never forget when I first heard Anjie lead worship at a woman's conference that Joni Ames was hosting through ACTS Ministry. Anjie was the featured worship leader. Anjie has an amazing voice, and from the first note she sings, the presence of God is ushered in. To have her at my house each week, leading worship, was a true gift to all of us. When we did have guests come to visit, she was very willing to step aside, but was still fully committed to us as a group to lead, guide, and direct as we were growing in the Spirit.

It was not long after we began our fall meetings that many opportunities came knocking at the door to host visitors from many different places. Early on with Jehovah-Shammah Ministries, I felt it was right to open the door to people from various walks in the Christian faith to come and share their testimony, gifts, and talents with us.

The first visitor we had in the fall of 2004 was Paul Ssembiro. I had met him a year earlier when Bishop Henry Ormobi had been in town, and now Paul was in town for a two-week visit. We were fortunate to be able to host and get to know him.

Paul Ssembiro

I can truly say that I have not met very many men like Paul Ssembiro. He is a most precious man of God who walks in humility, kindness, and love. He is a gentle spirit who loves the Word of God and knows it to be truth. He carries the presence of the Lord in a way I have not seen in many others. When you look into his face, you see Jesus: that's just the best way I can explain it. It is remarkable. Paul is gifted in a way that all who hear him preach know they have just encountered the risen Christ. It is a privilege and an honor to know him and to call him my friend.

When Paul visited our group, he brought his keyboard so we could worship together. It is electrifying to be with your brothers and sisters in Christ worshipping together. After an hour of worship, we then sat and listened as Paul talked about the power of worship and praise and its effect on strengthening our relationship with the Lord. He had us open our Bibles to Psalm 42:1-2: "As the deer pants for streams of water, so my soul pants for you, O God. My soul thirsts for God, for the living God." Paul said that as we seek the Lord and worship Him, it draws us into deeper levels of intimacy with Him. Psalm 42:7-8 says: "Deep calls to deep in the roar of your waterfalls; all your waves and breakers have swept over me. By day the Lord directs his love, at night his song is with me—a prayer to the God of my life." The Lord is continually wooing us to come closer to Him. He desires for us to yearn for Him. In Proverbs 8:17, Scripture tells us: "I love those who love me, and those who seek me find me." We have to spend time with God to get to know Him better, and Paul said there is no better way to grow more in love with the Lord than through worship and praise. We should desire to seek and know God with all our heart. "Blessed are they who keep his statutes and seek him with all their heart." (Ps. 119:2) It is up to us how far we want to go in our relationship with the Lord. Our response to the Lord will determine how deep and how far He will take us in our relationship with Him.

The following week Paul came back, and this time he taught on the Holy Spirit our Helper. He talked to us about the importance of being fully dependent on the Holy Spirit, and made it clear that we as believers are to be witnesses for Jesus. Paul said we can only be effective witnesses with the help of the Holy Spirit. Paul went on to say:

Jesus promised the Holy Spirit to us. John 14:15-20 says: "If you love me, you will obey what I command. And I will ask the Father, and he will give you another Counselor to be with you forever—the Spirit of truth. The world cannot accept him, because it neither sees him nor knows him. But you know him, for he lives with you and will be in you. I will not leave you as orphans; I will come to you. Before long, the world will not see me anymore, but you will see me. Because I live, you also will live. On that day you will realize that I am in my Father, and you are in me, and I am in you."

John 16:5-11 says: "Now that I am going to him who sent me, yet none of you asks me, 'Where are you going?' Because I have said these things, you are filled with grief. But I tell you the truth: It is for your good that I am going away. Unless I go away, the Counselor will not come to you; but if I go, I will send him to you. When he comes, he will convict the world of guilt in regard to sin and righteousness and judgment: in regard to sin, because men do not believe in me; in regard to righteousness, because I am going to the Father, where you can see me no longer; in regard to judgment, because the prince of this world now stands condemned."

The Holy Spirit is a person. He is the Spirit of truth and He is the Spirit of grace. He is part of the Trinity. He is to be worshipped. In Acts 13:2-3, we read: "While they were worshipping the Lord and fasting, the Holy Spirit said, 'Set apart for me Barnabas and Saul for the work to which I have called them.' So after they had fasted and prayed, they placed their hands on them and sent them off." The Holy Spirit should not be grieved. "Do not let any unwholesome talk come out of your mouths, but only what is helpful for building others up according to their needs, that it may benefit those who listen. And do not grieve the Holy Spirit of God, with whom you were sealed for the day of redemption." (Eph. 4:29-30)

We need to be indwelled by the Holy Spirit. He is a gift to the church and He comes into our lives when we ask Him. He won't go against our will but when we invite Him in, He comes. Luke 11:9-13 says: "So I say to you: Ask and it will be given to you; seek and you will find; knock and the door will be opened to you. For everyone who asks receives; he who seeks finds; and to him who knocks, the door will be opened. Which of you fathers, if your son asks for a fish, will give him a snake instead? Or if he asks for an egg, will give him a scorpion? If you then, though you are evil, know how to give good gifts to your children, how much more will your Father in heaven give the Holy Spirit to those who ask him!"

God was setting the stage. He desired for us to grow intimately in relationship with Him through worship and praise, and Anjie was in place to help us with that. The Lord also wanted us to understand who the Holy Spirit is so we could deepen our relationship with Him, and we were getting ready to hear testimony after testimony of how the Holy Spirit impacts lives. It was a perfect message as the fall season God had in store for us began to unfold.

John Scotland

The very next week, another opportunity presented itself. A man named John Scotland was in town and he had heard about our group through one of the women who had attended some of the meetings. He was free to come spend a morning with us and had heard about our enthusiasm and desire to know the Holy Spirit. Having never met the man, I prayed for the Lord's will in hosting him. The Lord answered "Yes" and then He said: "You are providing a new wine skin for new wine to be poured into." I later found out that John's ministry is called New Wine, but I also knew that this word from the Lord was a picture of what He was doing with us a group.

One of my favorite parables in the Bible is about the new wine skin. Matthew, Mark, and Luke all share this parable, but the Luke passage speaks the most to me. "No one tears a patch from a new garment and sews it on an old one. If he does, he will have torn the new garment, and the patch from the new will not match the old. And no one pours new wine into old wineskins. If he does, the new wine will burst the skins, the wine will run out and the wineskins will be ruined. No, new wine must be poured into new wineskins. And no one after drinking old wine wants the new, for he says, 'The old is better.'" (Luke 5:36-39)

This is a clear picture of what happens in a church when the new wine, the Holy Spirit, is poured out and lives are changed and new life is birthed. The new wine is likened to a new piece of cloth. When the new wine is being poured out, it must be put in a new wine skin. The new wine skin can represent a new mindset, a new willingness to receive the Holy Spirit, a new way of doing things. The new wine has to be received by people who are willing to put the old wine aside for the new. You cannot pour new wine into an old wineskin. The old wineskin is represented in the form of old mindsets, old structures, old set of rules and traditions, the old way of doing things. New wine will cause the old wineskin to burst. However, Scripture warns, people who have been drinking the old wine *think the old is better.* Those not willing to drink "the new wine" miss out on all the new wine the Holy Spirit has to offer.

When you encounter the Holy Spirit and allow Him in your life, you are changed. You become a new wine skin. John Scotland was just the person to push the envelope with us to help us move further away from our "old wineskin" mentality. He had new wine to share with us and we were more than willing to receive it.

John is from Liverpool, England. He is married to Jean and they have four children. John's ministry began in the '70s as he embarked upon healing and evangelistic tent meetings. He later became the pastor of a small church in Liverpool and was "recognized by the Queen of England and Prince Charles for his work with the poor and unemployed youth of the city." In 1994, John received a word from prophet Bobby Conner that changed his life. He received what he terms: "an anointing of intoxication of joy and drunkenness in the Holy Spirit." He now travels the globe to preach the Good News and offers hope, encouragement, and "spiritual refreshment" to the body of Christ.[3]

The morning began with John simply sharing his testimony. A testimony is a powerful tool. We read in Revelations 12:11 that we overcome the enemy, "by the blood of the Lamb [Jesus' sacrifice] and by the word of their testimony." 2 Corinthians 3:2-3 says that *we* are letters testifying to the Lord. "You show that you are a letter from Christ, the result of our ministry, written not with ink but with the Spirit of the living God, not on tablets of stone but on tablets of human hearts."

John read Ephesians 4:30 from *The Message* which says: "Don't grieve God. Don't break His heart. His Holy Spirit, moving and breathing in you, is the most intimate part of your life, making you fit for himself. Don't take such a gift for granted." Wow! You could sit and ponder that verse for hours. John shared this particular verse because he had a major encounter with the Holy Spirit that took him out of his comfort zone. He said it took him out of the realm of himself. "The anointing of the Holy Spirit comes with offense, which comes from our own defense. We build a wall around our hearts to keep people out and in the process, we keep the Holy Spirit out. When we are offended by people, it's like we are hitting the fence we ourselves have built up. *Ouch*! And the Lord wants us to get '*over* the *fence*'—over the offense. When we do, we come into a bigger realm of the Spirit with much bigger boundaries," he said.

And when the anointing of the Holy Spirit came over John, he began to do things naturally that he would have never done before. One time he said he began to sing a Beatles song during a sermon, which was not the way he was used to delivering a sermon! He asked God why this was happening. And the Lord said, "You are prophesying in a secular mode to the Church because I am doing a new thing in the midst of My people. My people have had My Word for years, but they've done nothing with it. They have worshipped My Word, but are doing nothing with it. They have not allowed My Word to take root in their heart, so now, I am going to send you, John, as an offense, to upset My people."

John then shared a story about being on his deck at home and seeing a bumble bee going from one flower to another. John said the Lord began to speak to him. "John, My move is going to be like that of a bumble bee." John went on to explain what he understood the Lord meant: "Now ladies, this is an interesting word for you all this morning because the name Deborah means 'bee.' Deborah was a leader. She was a prophetess. She was a judge. There is an anointing being released here today. The tradition of the church as a whole is that men are the leaders. But here is the prophetic thing about the bee: if the next move of God is going to look like a bee, well, bees break all the aerodynamic rules. It should not be able to fly. Its body is too big for its wings. I believe God is going to do something amongst us that will break all of our concepts of how God should move. He is wider and deeper and higher than we can grasp. We have to get into the flow of the Spirit. The Spirit is the Spirit of revelation, and He can do some crazy things. It is crazy because we don't understand. Once we understand, it is not crazy anymore. I believe in the last times, an anointing of God will be released for all the ladies to come into all the fullness God has for you. There is no male or female in the Spirit. (Gal. 3:28) Now *that* is breaking the rules! Also, a bee cross-pollinates. In the West, you have to send a church a tape so they can hear you speak before they will invite you to visit. In Africa, the pulpits are open. They are begging you to come and share the Gospel. Everything is possible with God. Nothing is impossible. Nothing is impossible."

It was a powerful word to hear. It was also very encouraging and many of the women who were at the meeting that day were especially blessed as they felt the Lord was talking directly to them. Some of the women had been in churches where they had not been allowed to operate in their gifting and calling. This word gave all of us hope and vision for the future—belief that we would be able to walk in our destiny.

John went on and shared a bit more about himself and told some more stories about how the Holy Spirit was moving. He ended the meeting by asking us to line up from tallest to shortest so he could begin to prophetically minister to us individually. It was outrageous and fun and we laughed and had the best time. Can you imagine, having fun receiving ministry? The Holy Spirit does have a sense of humor. When John got to a woman who was standing behind me in the line, he started saying: "Ding dong, ding dong, special delivery, special delivery." We laughed and laughed wondering what in the world that could mean? I did not even know the woman. She was a guest, a friend of a friend. Yet God is extremely detailed in putting things together. Really, there are not words to describe His pinpoint planning, and what we all learned that day was our Father in Heaven is a fun God who loves to laugh and enjoy time with us. We just need to be willing to be open to receive *all* of who He is. You will read later on in Chapter 10 just what this word John spoke meant.

Another thing I was beginning to understand was the meaning of the Scripture in Matthew 7: "you will know them by their fruit." John's ministry and way the Holy Spirit operates through him has been criticized over the years. Critics have accused him of not operating under the unction of the Holy Spirit. But what I learned is that the real testimony to his authenticity is in the fruit of his ministry. "By their fruit you will recognize them. Do people pick grapes from thornbushes, or figs from thistles? Likewise every good tree bears good fruit, but a bad tree bears bad fruit. A good tree cannot bear bad fruit, and a bad tree cannot bear good fruit. Every tree that does not bear good fruit is cut down and thrown into the fire. Thus, by their fruit you will recognize them." (Matt. 7:16-20)

For days and weeks after John's visit, I received phone calls from women who had attended the meeting and been blessed by John, his teaching and his ministry. We ended up hosting him again several more times and still have a relationship with him to this day. Knowing him has been a wonderful blessing.

Nick Herbert

In September, the group hosted a new friend named Nick Herbert. Nick was in town visiting from St. Mary's Church in London, England where he was one of the key worship leaders. Nick was invited by a group in Charlotte who had come together to discern whether or not John Peters, now the Vicar of St Mary's, was to plant a church here in Charlotte. The discernment process initially began with prayer and had now evolved into more serious talks about a church plant. Consequently, St. Mary's agreed to send over worship leaders, teachers, and preachers from their church to Charlotte on a monthly basis to aid in this process. Our little home prayer group was going to get to reap the benefits of these visits.

Nick was a delight. We spent this particular morning mostly in worship, singing, and praising the Lord together. Nick also encouraged us to sing in tongues and the melody and spontaneous worship was absolutely lovely. "Sing joyfully to the Lord, you righteous; it is fitting for the upright to praise him. Praise the Lord with harp; make music to him on the ten-stringed lyre. Sing to him a new song; play skillfully, and shout for joy." (Ps. 33:1-3)

Nick then spent the rest of the morning sharing a message from Matthew 25:14-30, the parable of the talents:

> "Again, it will be like a man going on a journey, who called his servants and entrusted his property to them. To one he gave five talents of money, to another two talents, and to another one talent, each according to his ability. Then he went on his journey. The man who had received the five talents went at once

and put his money to work and gained five more. So also, the one with two talents gained two more. But the man who had received the one talent went off, dug a hole in the ground and hid his master's money. After a long time the master of those servants returned and settled accounts with them. The man who had received the five talents brought the other five. 'Master,' he said, 'you entrusted me with five talents. See, I have gained five more.' His master replied, 'Well done, good and faithful servant! You have been faithful with a few things; I will put you in charge of many things. Come and share your master's happiness!' The man with the two talents also came. 'Master,' he said, 'you entrusted me with two talents; see, I have gained two more.' His master replied, 'Well done, good and faithful servant! You have been faithful with a few things; I will put you in charge of many things. Come and share your master's happiness!' Then the man who had received the one talent came. 'Master,' he said, 'I knew that you are a hard man, harvesting where you have not sown and gathering where you have not scattered seed. So I was afraid and went out and hid your talent in the ground. See, here is what belongs to you.' His master replied, 'You wicked, lazy servant! So you knew that I harvest where I have not sown and gather where I have not scattered seed? Well then, you should have put my money on deposit with the bankers, so that when I returned I would have received it back with interest. Take the talent from him and give it to the one who has the ten talents. For everyone who has will be given more, and he will have an abundance. Whoever does not have, even what he has will be taken from him. And throw that worthless servant outside, into the darkness, where there will be weeping and gnashing of teeth."

Nick encouraged us as a group to be faithful with the things God was giving us, not to bury the blessings but to invest them and multiply them. He encouraged us to take the Lord's calling on our lives and the gifts He gives us, the opportunities He gives us, and run with it! The two in the parable who heard the call, made the most with what they had. Then Nick asked, "Are you making the most with what God has entrusted to you?"

He spoke to us about how our lives are to be a response to God's phone call. "What do you do when the phone rings?' Nick asked us. "Do you mute it, do you put it in your back pocket for another time to respond, or do you answer it?" Nick encouraged us that day to take the call and run with it. That is when the Lord can multiply things. "The heart of a dynamic Christian is to respond to God's phone call— God's revelation, and then you are supposed to do something with it. We don't want it to be our story," Nick continued, "we want it to be His story. We have an obvious calling. We read it in the Book. We are to heal the sick, cast out demons, and preach the Good News. If we are not doing these things, then what are we doing? It is time to walk in worship and lose the fear of doing it right or wrong. It is not about doing it right or wrong. You've got to trust. You've got to trust the Lord. The wise ones in the parable risked it all because they knew their Master and they trusted him. It's time to trust the Lord and, as the Nike commercial says, 'Just do it!'" Nick said it again: "Just do it!"

This parable in Matthew 25 makes me think of the mustard seed again. I wonder how many times the Lord gives out mustard seeds and we choose not to invest them but bury them, for fear we may make a mistake. This word really challenged us to go on and invest our time and talent on the seed opportunities the Lord gives us. May we all be good stewards of those opportunities the Lord places in our hands and along our path.

We ended the meeting with a time of ministry and Nick was able to pray over each person and bless each one with a word from the Lord. It was a wonderful morning and another time of refreshing and conviction.

You learn that the Lord's ways are not necessarily our ways. "'For my thoughts are not your thoughts, neither are your ways my ways,' declares the Lord. 'As the heavens are higher than the earth, so are my ways higher than your ways and my thoughts than your thoughts.'" (Isa. 55:8-9) We were watching the Lord creatively arrange our meeting times and the messages He had for us to hear. His purpose was to train us so that we could begin to operate in the Spirit and in ways to advance His kingdom and He was blessing us all at the same time.

Reflection

As you become a new wine skin, ask the Lord to change your old mindsets so you can receive the new wine in abundance. This is an on-going process. Paul, John, and Nick had all talked about life in the Spirit, and challenged us to open ourselves up to Him. As the Holy Spirit becomes more alive in your life, and as you open yourself up to more of the things of the Spirit, trust the Lord. And have faith. God is a God of the supernatural, and as you just read in Isaiah 55, His ways can be very different than ours at times. If you are being challenged in ways that are new and maybe even uncomfortable to you, go talk with someone who is mature in the life of the Holy Spirit. Talk openly with them about your feelings, concerns, and worries. Go get a book about the Holy Spirit or do a word study from a concordance, such as *Strong's Concordance*. Branch out and explore. Living life with the Holy Spirit is like going on a daily treasure hunt. There is a lifetime's worth of things to explore and treasure to find. Invest your time in the Spirit. The rewards will be both present and eternal.

Prayer

Holy Spirit come. I know that at times Your ways can seem strange, mysterious, and even scary. But Lord, I want to know more about You and I want to be a good a faithful servant with all that You have given to me. I want to hear You say, "Well done." Help me today think outside of the box of my understanding, outside of the box of my tradition, outside of the box of my experience so I can experience You, Holy Spirit, in a whole new way. Please bring along my path people who can mentor me in the things of the Spirit. And as I pray, I thank You in advance Lord that You will show me what is of You and what is not. I ask these things in Jesus' Name. Amen

Suggested Bible Readings

All of Isaiah 55; Colossians 3:16-17, 23-24; 4:2-6

Other Books

There is a true story of the Holy Spirit changing the course of history in the early 1900s. *The Azusa Street Revival* by Robert Liardon is worth the read and will give you some understanding of how the Holy Spirit operates.

Experiencing the Spirit by Robert Heidler
They Speak In Other Tongues by John L. Sherrill
Acts of The Holy Spirit: God's Power For Living by Lloyd J. Ogilvie

CHAPTER 9

The Outpouring: Part 2

Jonny Grant and Paul Sawry

OCTOBER CAME AND SO DID two more new guests. Jonny Grant and Paul Sawry from St. Mary's Church were in town. I met them at dinner the weekend they arrived. Jonny's first words to me were: "You're Anne! Your reputation and the reputation of the women's group precede you. All Nick has talked about is the meeting in your home." It seemed that Nick was as blessed by us as we were by him, and had gone back to London to share about what the Lord was doing at our meetings. How exciting for us to hear the Lord was using us to bless others.

I invited Jonny and Paul to come to our home meeting the

following Tuesday and they accepted. Paul was a worship leader at St. Mary's and Jonny was on staff as head of the Pastoral Department. We began the morning as usual, with worship. Paul introduced us to a beautiful song we had never heard before, called "The Wine of the Kingdom." As we learned the words and sang them, we began to see that they had a prophetic implication and presented a prophetic picture of what God was doing with us as a group. Here are some of the lyrics:

> One shall tell another
> And he shall tell his friend
> Husbands, wives, and children
> Shall come following on
> From house to house in families
> Shall more be gathered in
> And lights will shine in every street
> So warm and welcoming.

> **Refrain:**
> Come on in and taste the new wine
> The wine of the Kingdom
> The wine of the Kingdom of God
> Here is healing and forgiveness
> The wine of the Kingdom
> The wine of the Kingdom of God.[4]

© 1981 Kingsway Thankyou Music

Once again, the Lord inhabited the praises of His people and when the worship time was over, Jonny shared a message he felt the Lord had for us. He read from Acts 2:42-47: "They devoted themselves to the apostle's teaching and to the fellowship, to the breaking of bread and to prayer. Everyone was filled with awe, and many wonders and miraculous signs were done by the apostles. All the believers were together and had everything in common. Selling their possessions and goods, they gave to anyone as he had need. Every day they continued to meet together in the temple courts. They broke bread in their homes and ate together with glad and sincere hearts, praising God and enjoying the favor of all the people. *And the Lord added to their number daily those who were being saved."* (Emphasis added.)

Jonny said we should be encouraged by what God was doing with us as a group, and not to underestimate what was happening. He reminded us that God is bigger than any of our expectations and He would give to us much more than we would know to ask for. Jonny then began to speak prophetically over us:

> God will add to and bless this time. As you continue to meet, meeting people's needs, eating, and praying together, God will add to this and it will become an attractive place with God in the center. As you faithfully continue to meet and wait patiently, you will be like an oasis in a dry desert. This time will be refreshing and as you look to God and meet together, seeking Him and worshipping Him, people will see this place as an oasis. Don't be surprised if God develops and grows it. God is at work here. Trust Him. Let things naturally unfold, take form and shape. He who has begun a good work will see it to completion. (Phil 1:6) This is a genuine community—it is the forming of the Body of Christ. You will discover what your gifts are and the way that happens is through getting to know one another. There may be some resistance to what God is doing because it is shaking up something that does not want to be shaken up and hasn't been shaken up in a long time. When pressure comes, it is great to be a team.

Then something unexpected happened. Jonny began to share, openly and honestly, his personal story, specifically about the infertility issue he and his wife Esther were going through, and he shared in detail the heartache they had been enduring. There was a holy hush in the room as Jonny opened his heart to us. At the end of his sharing,

Anjie stepped forward and said she felt she had a word of encouragement for Jonny. She began to minister to him, prophesying life and renewed vision for him and Esther. As the Holy Spirit gave her, and then others, the words to pray, the rest of the group began praying in tongues in intercession. Anjie was led to break curses off the family line and prayed for a release from past generational bondage. She even went on to say the following: "I am going out on a limb here but I believe the Spirit is saying that a baby is on the horizon it will be a girl." Several of the women kept hearing or seeing in their minds eye the number eight. The number eight in the prophetic means "new beginnings."

As the prayer time wrapped up, Jonny said he felt God had "ambushed" him. He said he had no idea he would be sharing his own personal story with us. It was wonderful for us to bless him that day as he and Paul had so blessed us. It was a shift, and a new beginning for the group. Remember the number eight? It was not only a word for Jonny, but a word for the group as well. New beginnings. From that meeting on, our women's prayer group began ministering to every speaker that came through the door to teach us.

We would have to wait a while to see the fruit of that day's ministry with Jonny. But as God would have it, we did have another opportunity to see Jonny again and on that visit, we got to meet Esther. And sure enough, Jonny and Esther ended up conceiving and delivering a beautiful, healthy baby girl. They named her Ruby. My, what a mighty God we serve!

Latha Ramesh Pandian

It is kind of hard for me to believe that the very next week, we hosted another guest. Her name was Latha Ramesh Pandian, and she was a missionary from Kuwait. Never could I have conjured up or made this opportunity happen. Latha was acquainted with Anjie and she was in town visiting her friend, Sally Reep. When Anjie asked if

Latha could come spend the morning with us, I quickly said yes. To spend a morning with a missionary from Kuwait sounded fascinating. What unfolded was truly remarkable.

Latha is originally from India. She accepted Jesus at age ten. She is married to Ramesh Pandian. She had met Sally at a MorningStar conference in 1998, and had been back to the States thirteen times to visit. She is a mother of two, and she and her husband co-Pastor a church in Kuwait called the Vineyard Ministry (not associated with the Vineyard church in the US.)

Latha is gifted prophetically and from the moment she began to speak, the presence of the Lord was in the room. Below is what she shared with us. You can imagine our great surprise when she had us open our Bibles to Judges 5:7 to read about Deborah. You will recall, the Lord had John Scotland share a similar word with us a month earlier.

Latha opened with a powerful, lengthy, anointed prayer. Some key phrases of the prayer were: "Change us Lord. Soak us, O God. Transform us. Make us to be like a trumpet. Shake us that we would be totally changed and transformed. We need You here. We are hungry for Your presence, O God, and Your fire. Come and meet us with Your suddenlies, with Your surprises." Latha then began her talk.

"There are many generals in this place. God's generals. God wants to take you in His chariots of fire as never before. God is counting on you for the nations. God is giving many of you skating shoes. God is choosing you. God will energize you for what you have to do. He will use you to change the atmosphere. Each and every one of you is here for a purpose, and each one of you is needed by God. Go to Judges 5:7," Latha continued. "Village life in Israel ceased, ceased until I, Deborah, arose, arose a mother in Israel."(Judg. 5:7) Then Latha began to share a bit of her personal testimony.

> In October 1997, a small group of intercessors met in a home and we were calling on the Lord. He manifested Himself, and came down as gold dust all over the room. We did not know if

this was the Lord or the devil. Then I came to MorningStar in 1998 and found out that what we were experiencing was true! I went back the strangest woman in India. The presence of God continued to increase, so much so that when we met, it was strange to many. But the small group in our home grew into a church. Many were questioning and doubting the church, and some left. But the anointing breaks the yoke. Many came to the Lord.

God is calling us to come up to a higher place from where we are. Arise! Get up! Arise from your position; arise from your bondage. Come to the royal priesthood. Come up, stand up, *Arise!*

Now Deborah means "bee." Bees have a stinger. So the enemy is afraid of you. You should not be afraid of the enemy, in Jesus' Name. Nothing happens in your family to cause you to lose your joy—do not be afraid. God has His hand on you. So you need to stand tall in the presence of your enemy. You need to stand up tall in the presence of sickness, in *all* opposition. You will never bow because *you are a Deborah! You are a Deborah!*

Deborah was responsible for bringing peace to a big nation. She was a judge. She was judging Israel as a prophetess. God is sending you—you are a prophetess. You do not know what you have inside of you. Rise up to that placement, that new position, that new responsibility, that new healing.

Deborah was a housewife who was hearing God. So me and my household—Lord, if You've got me in Your hand, me and my household will serve You! (Josh. 24:15) Me and my children, we will serve You, Lord. Me and my generations, we will serve You. We bless them and break any curses that have come upon them. We stand tall with our stinger, and we go and interfere in all the work the enemy has done in our families, in Jesus' Name. And we take the generations back for God's Kingdom.

The foundation—the beginning of what I needed to do is to stand in the gap because I know my position. If I open up my mouth and speak a word—it will come to pass. If I bless, the blessing will stay because I am a prophetic judge. When I make a declaration, that declaration will be the rule of the land—the law of the land. I can change a situation. *Awake, awake* Deborah!

The hissing noise that bees make—so many bees gather together and there is so much noise. It is a song of deliverance, a song of freedom. When I open my mouth, let it be a positive voice, not a negative one. I will not utter fear. I will utter faith in my mouth. In all things, I want to speak positives over my home and my family. Don't begin your day looking at what you do not have.

Go to Ephesians 1:17, and you, a servant, a prophet, an intercessor, pray to the Father of Glory. "I keep asking that the God of our Lord Jesus Christ, the glorious Father, may give you the Spirit of wisdom and revelation, so that you may know him better." God, will You bring Your glory, Your light into the darkness? Grant insight into Your mysteries and Your secrets, O God. Lord, we want an eye opening to see Your mysteries because You are the God of glory, and You have a heart flooded with light. So let my heart be flooded with Your light.

Bees are busy all the time. In the church, we need different types of bees. One bee does nothing else but stand at the entrance of the hive and fan its wings. That is their job. These kinds of bees will stand before the Lord and ask for the fresh bread to come upon the church.

Then there are cleansing bees. Their duty is to intercede for cleansing sake. They will intercede for the leaders, for families. They connect people to holiness. Wherever you are, you can intercede as the Lord directs you. Don't you think our nations need cleansing?

Bees are mindful of their business, and they don't get involved in the other busyness around them. I think you all have maybe heard all of this before. But this is what the Lord is putting on my heart to share with you today. God is encouraging you today. You have a role to play, and it is a very simple role to play, Amen. You can do it!

Then there are queen bees. They are the ones who bring many bees, many children, into the hive. They birth them. Lord, give us the birthing anointing so we will birth things to come to life. The anointing of the Lord can look chaotic. We should not be afraid of the anointing of the Lord, even though it can look very different and strange at times. The anointing is like honey. When situations get worse, ask the Lord for more of His anointing, more honey. We will feel great pressure in our lives; therefore, we need a greater anointing. Soak in the honey. Soak in Him. Tell Him your needs. Stay in His presence until His fragrance is on you.

In order for Abraham to be called the father of faith, he had to get up from where he was and go. Get up, by faith, and walk out to the place the Lord directs you to. He is directing you to a place of freedom! *Arise*, Deborah, *arise!* You know the prophetic anointing needs a life of intimacy with Jesus. All the time, Jesus should be on our minds. Then it makes it easy for us to hear Him when He has something to say to us. It is time to come out of all the busyness to listen to Him and hear Him, to walk with Him.

Then, Latha closed in prayer:

Lord, we declare there is no man in this world that can take Your place. Come Lord, kiss us with the kiss of Your lips. Our spirits are open. Our hearts are ready. We want a fresh kiss from You. Come Lord. Intimacy. Relationship. Obedience. Queen Vashti could not obey the king. But Esther did. O God, I want to enter into Your presence like that. I want to hear Your voice say, "Queen Esther."

The Lord says, "If I am called the King of Glory, then you are Queen." The Queen is decorated gloriously from within. Come, decorate us O God. Give that fresh fire unto us, O God. Consume us, O God. Help us to develop a deeper intimacy with You. There is no one like You, O God. No one can take Your place. Let me fall in love with You all over again. Jesus come. Change our position today from daughters of Zion into the Shulammite position. (See Song of Sol. 6:13) Shulammite will seek You, go with You, love You, birth for You, stand up and call to You.

Take us closer to Your heart, Lord. We want to tell You, we surrender our lives to You. Come, Lord, Come.

(Note: Shulammite means "the beloved." Song of Solomon 6:13 says: "Come back, come back, O Shulammite; come back, come back, that we may gaze on you!")

John Scotland, a man from Liverpool who had never met us before, had called us Deborahs and now, a woman from Kuwait was doing the same thing. Nick Herbert had said, "Just do it!" and Latha was encouraging us to get out there and do it. Paul Ssembiro had talked to us about deepening our relationship with the Lord through worship and Jonny had talked to us about the pressure that comes when we move further in our relationship with the God through the Holy Spirit. Latha was encouraging us to "soak in the honey," when that pressure happens. Soak in the presence of the Lord. God had heard our prayer and was sending teachers and Spiritual fathers and mothers to our group to call us to life, to give us a push to move out and to spur us on in our walk with the Holy Spirit. I don't know about you, but I think that is pretty spectacular. But then again, God is a pretty spectacular God.

Alan Smith

The following week, we hosted a wonderful man whose name is Alan Smith. Alan is Anjie's spiritual Daddy, and she invited him to come visit us. He is a full time dairy farmer and president of Daddy Pete Farms in Stony Point, NC. In addition to his work as a farmer, Alan is an inspirational teacher, speaker, and leader. Alan is also the founder of Stony Point Christian Publications (SPCP), an organization dedicated to acknowledging the presence and activity of God in our world. This ministry focuses on supporting churches, ministries, and intercessors, and one way that happens is through the publication, "Thoughts and Perceptions."[5] We were so happy to finally meet him as Anjie had talked a lot about him. We found him to be a man of humility, compassion, and one who had deep reverence for the Lord.

Alan began the morning by sharing part of his testimony with us. He told us about his upbringing and when he came to know Jesus. He shared about his family. He told us about his diagnosis with lung cancer, and how the Lord used that illness to show Alan that He still heals today. Yes, the Lord healed Alan of lung cancer. He shared about the months he spent with the Lord during his illness, and the process he went through as the Lord began to heal his body. It is a powerful story of the healing nature of God, which is still at work today.

Alan then directed his talk to us. He had us write down the following sentence. "God is always working behind the scenes on my behalf." Alan suggested that the reason all of us were together meeting as a group was because God did something behind the scenes on our behalf that resulted in the birth of the Tuesday prayer group. None of us had ever thought of it that way. Then he said, "Once you begin to discover that God has been behind the scenes working on your behalf, you will begin to see that there will be times you get moved quickly and supernaturally from one place of knowing Him to another, and when you look back, you will wonder, "how in the world did I get here?" It is because as we invite Him into our lives, the Lord will begin to move us forward in our relationship with Him, sometimes much faster than you could have anticipated."

We then opened our Bibles to 2 Peter 1:1-11, and Alan began to teach on the divine nature and God's divine power.

> Simon Peter, a servant and apostle of Jesus Christ, says to those who through the righteousness of our God and Savior Jesus Christ have received a faith as precious as ours: Grace and peace be yours in abundance through the knowledge of God and of Jesus our Lord. His divine power has given us everything we need for life and godliness through our knowledge of him who

called us by his own glory and goodness. Through these he has given us his very great and precious promises, so that through them you may participate in the divine nature and escape the corruption in the world caused by evil desires. For this very reason, make every effort to add to your faith goodness; and to goodness, knowledge; and to knowledge, self-control; and to self-control, perseverance; and to perseverance, godliness; and to godliness, brotherly kindness; and to brotherly kindness, love. For if you possess these qualities in increasing measure, they will keep you from being ineffective and unproductive in your knowledge of our Lord Jesus Christ. But if anyone does not have them, he is nearsighted and blind, and has forgotten that he has been cleansed from his past sins. Therefore, my brothers, be all the more eager to make your calling and election sure. For if you do these things, you will never fall, and you will receive a rich welcome into the eternal kingdom of our Lord and Savior Jesus Christ.

Alan suggested that it was God's divine power that got us to where we were even though five years ago, none of us would have foreseen that we would have been gathered together in a group meeting in October 2004. Verse 4 says God's divine power produces a promise so that we can participate in the divine nature. We can be partakers of the same divine nature *right now* that we are going to have when we get to heaven. "For His divine power has bestowed upon us all things that are requisite and suited to life and godliness, through the full, personal knowledge of Him Who called us by *and* to His own glory and excellent virtue. By means of these He has bestowed on us His precious and exceedingly great promises, so that through them you may escape by flight from the moral decay, rottenness and corruption that is in the world because of covetousness, lust and greed, *and become sharers, partakers of the divine nature.*" (2 Pet. 1:3-4 AMP) (Emphasis added.) Alan continued:

"Jesus prayed a prayer: 'Our Father, who art in heaven, hallowed by thy Name. Thy Kingdom come, thy will be done on earth as it is in heaven.' What is Jesus talking about? He is talking about the divine nature. So God has taken us from point A to point B and taken us from a place we can never return to because He is pouring into each of us by His power the nature people in heaven have in fullness. He desires to pour into each of us His divine nature. All we have to do is respond, yield to Him. God will come along and impart something of the Spirit in us and all I am doing is putting to words what it is I see that the Lord is doing here with you. The nature of heaven is the nature of Jesus. What makes heaven heaven? Everyone in heaven has the divine nature of God. So what makes your time together as a group a little like heaven? It's because you are sitting in here now with some of the divine nature operating in you. Jesus lives in each one of you, so that means the divine nature does too."

Alan then had us write down another sentence. "There's not necessarily a blessed place. You are a blessed people."

"So it's important to understand that you are blessed wherever you are," he continued. "Christ lives in you so it is not about where you are meeting; it is about understanding that Jesus is in you wherever you are. He sees you, loves you, and encounters you. He thinks you're a ten! In God's eyes, you are perfect. He loves you where you are and He's got you where you are and He will take you the rest of the way."

"At best," Alan said, "we are all playing T-ball." Alan shared a dream he had where he was sitting in the bleachers with Jesus, watching a T-ball game. Every time a kid would get up and swing and miss the ball, Jesus would say, "Good job, good job." Alan said he asked the Lord why He was saying "good job" when the kids were not even hitting the ball, and Jesus replied, "Because they are trying to do it for Me." Alan reminded us we don't have to get it right all the time in order for it to count in Jesus' eyes. A religious spirit tells us we have to do it all right and do it right all the time. That's not the way Jesus operates. What's important is that we are trying.

Alan ended his talk by reminding us we were all at different mile markers in the faith; we were all at a different places on the road. "The scenery will look different to each of you," he said. "As Christians, we need to learn to appreciate where everyone is on their journey and realize the Lord places us where He wants us to be. 1 Corinthians 12:18 says: 'God has arranged the parts in the body, every one of them, just as he wanted them to be.' So we all are going to look different. The key," he said, "is respecting everyone where they are."

Alan eventually became the overseer of our prayer group. A kind and gentle man, we were blessed to have him take an interest in our group and take us under his wing. We had been praying for someone to come along beside us who was mature in the Lord, and His influence over the years has been instrumental helping us grow up to be Spirit-led women of God.

It is interesting to note here that not too long after Alan's visit, I began getting that "sense" again in my spirit that a change was coming. It had to be strange having that thought back then as I ponder it now and look at all that was going on. But the Lord has His timing and His ways of doing things. If you, the reader, don't take away anything else from reading this story, remember that the flow of the Holy Spirit is *life*, and if you surrender yourself to Him, you will enjoy the greatest adventure of all. I asked the Lord to show me how to move forward and told Him that I was still on board for whatever He had in mind. I was still willing to open my home to be a gathering place for this body of women if that was what He wanted me to continue to do, and I simply believed He would make it clear and that I would hear.

Reflection

Deborah has a unique story. So do you. As a woman, Deborah had a high calling in her life. She loved the Lord and served Him well. I hope her story will inspire you, whether you are male or female. Begin to see yourself for the special person that you are. There is a calling in your life. Do you know what it is? Have you ever asked the Lord to show you? Maybe today is the day to begin realizing this truth. Ask the Lord to show you what it is He has called you to do in the Body of Christ. And if you are already walking in your calling, ask Him to show you how to move into a deeper understanding and conviction of that calling so you don't miss out on anything He has designed for you to do to further His kingdom.

Prayer

Thank You Lord, that You have called me and that I have a purpose to advance Your kingdom here on earth. I desire to walk in the fullness of my calling. I want to be all it is You have created me to be. Thank You that Your handprint is in me. May all the treasures You deposited in me to be an effective life-giver and world-changer be released so I can walk in Your ways to the glory of Your name. Lord, I do not want to bury any opportunity You give to me to venture out in. Help me to be willing to take the risk—to take the next step. Help me learn to trust You more, believing You are behind the scenes on my behalf preparing the way. Help me to *"just do it"* Lord. I want to do it all for You! I ask this in Jesus' Name. Amen.

Suggested Bible Readings

Judges 4 and 5; Ephesians 4:1-16

CHAPTER 10

The Outpouring: Part 3

Melissa Tyson

IN NOVEMBER, WE MET A precious girl named Melissa Tyson (now Melissa Tyson Upham—yep, she got married!) A friend of Anjie's, Melissa was in town visiting, so we invited her to come spend a Tuesday morning with our group. Melissa is a beautiful woman of the Lord and a very gifted one as well in many areas of the Spirit and in the natural world too. She is a gifted metal smith who creates the most beautiful jewelry—exquisite rings, necklaces, bracelets, earrings, and belt buckles to name a few, and she writes Scripture verses into each piece she makes.

We had the best time getting to know her as she told us how

the Lord wooed her into relationship with Him. Melissa shared part of her testimony with us, saying the Lord chased her around the world and back trying to get her to open her eyes to Him. In her testimony, she said the Lord spoke to her through many people and through many different ways: through her younger sister, through art school friends in Italy, through her cousin who gave her worship music to listen to as she traveled cross country in the U.S. Later, in the streets of London, Melissa said she had an encounter with an angel. But after reading the book, *Left Behind*, Melissa realized Jesus was who she had been looking for all along. At age twenty-three, she gave her life to the Lord.

The Lord eventually confirmed His plans for her when she heard a preacher preach a sermon from Exodus 31:3-5 which says: "And I have filled him with the Spirit of God, with skill, ability and knowledge in all kinds of crafts—to make artistic designs for work, in gold, silver and bronze, to cut and set stones." She said she knew right then that her talent for metal smithing was a gift the Lord gave her to honor Him. Art and jewelry making became a way of worship for her, she said, and we ended up enjoying an impromptu shopping day as Melissa shared her beautiful jewelry with us.

After the Show

By this time, we had begun having potluck lunches together after the meetings. These lunches began to take on a life of their own. Each week we would sit around my big farm table after a meeting and enjoy a good meal together. We termed this time "after the show." What started out being a time to just hang out, eat, and visit soon became another opportunity for the Holy Spirit to train us. We began sharing individual dreams we were having, and as we tuned our ear to one another and to the Spirit, we began to have the faith to step out and interpret one another's dreams. Anjie was very helpful with this as she had many more years' experience interpreting dreams than we had. Sitting around the table each week, sharing dreams and visions, gave us opportunity to learn how to interpret the symbolism in our dreams as we would piece together the meaning. At times we would understand that we were to intercede on behalf of a situation or a person, maybe for the city, for the church, or maybe for a family member. At other times, we would see God's correction for a situation and pray through that, standing in the gap and repenting. Several times, the joy of the Lord hit us and we just laughed and laughed. Sometimes, we would experience a Holy presence so palpable, no one could move or talk. And when His fragrance would enter the room—well, it is overwhelming to say the least. These are just a few examples of what would happen during our "after the show" time. It became just as special as the meeting times. The Lord seemed to honor every minute we gathered together in His name.

Now just in case you are interested, the key is for a great potluck is for each person to bring their favorite dish. Every time we decided to have lunch, I would send out an email, sometimes with suggestions and at other times, asking for input. Everyone would "reply all" to let the group know who was bringing what. Sometimes, one woman would decide to make a large pot of soup, so the rest of us would simply fill in with food to go along with soup. Sometimes we would have a big salad, and other times, homemade sandwiches. Many times the women went all out and made special desserts or side dishes. I tell you, we had some delicious meals. It was always a feast and a great time!

As a result of the training we were receiving, we were becoming a functioning body. Our group and meetings became known as a safe place for women to come and receive ministry, a place they could come share their hurts, their pains, their sorrows, and a place where they could receive prayer for healing. God was weaving together a beautiful tapestry with an eclectic bunch of ladies who all had one desire and one desire only—to go deeper into relationship with God the Father, God the Son, and God the Holy Spirit. It was turning out to be quite an amazing year as we bonded with the Lord and with one another. The Lord was not only teaching us, but using us. We were all so very thankful.

Kimber Britner / Jonny and Esther Grant

As the year came to a close, we had a wonderful opportunity to see Jonny Grant again and also meet his wife Esther. They were in town for another meeting about potentially starting a new church, and once again, we had the benefit of being able to host them on Tuesday morning.

Kimber Britner, one of Anjie's friends, also joined us this particular morning to lead worship. Kimber has a powerful testimony of her own. In the short version, she moved to Hollywood at age eighteen to pursue an acting career. She fell in love, got married, and moved to New England. She and Bill had four children. Then, at age thirty-six, her husband Bill was diagnosed with brain cancer and a mere five weeks later, he passed away. The rest of her testimony is one of healing, restoration, and the tenacious work of discovering her purpose, vision, and recreating her life. She moved to Charlotte and after being a single mom for seven years, met and married Mark. She then became certified to teach workshops helping other women find their purpose and vision in life. She and her family are now back in Los Angeles, California, where she is the President of Moxie Me Institute. "Through Moxie Me Institute she works with ready-for-success women who want to take their gifts out of hiding with a strategic plan for business success. After years of working with women, she discovered that once a woman grabs a hold of her vision she needs the tools and support to implement it. Now Kimber helps women own their moxie, leverage their unique brilliance, and live into purposeful vision."[6]

After a time of worship with Kimber leading, we turned the floor over to Esther. We were thrilled to meet her in person, having heard all about her from Jonny on his first visit with us. Esther captivated us with the story of her life. She told us how the Lord rescued her from darkness that was present in her childhood and teen years and brought hope, healing, and wholeness to her as He ushered her into His light through His Son Jesus and through healing prayer ministry. We were riveted by her story as she shared intimate, personal parts of her life, all the while testifying to God's faithfulness. What became even more moving and awe inspiring to us was that God had used our women's prayer group to play a small part in her overall healing.

Esther's personal journey for wholeness continued even after she and Jonny married, and this particular morning, Esther was able to share how things came into alignment as never before during the time Jonny was meeting us for the first time in Charlotte. As she told us about things that had transpired, we began to see how God had orchestrated, to a crescendo, many years of prayer.

While Esther was in England in October, the same time Jonny was in Charlotte spending the morning with us, her parents were in New Zealand. All of them were receiving ministry and revelation for wholeness, not only for themselves, but for the entire family. The Lord used the ministry time with Jonny in Charlotte to confirm and bless all that was going on behind the scenes in England and New Zealand.

What helped solidify everything was a tape I had made during the prayer ministry time with Jonny when he was with us. Immediately after his visit, I felt prompted to send it to Esther so she could hear all the prayers that had been prayed over Jonny when he was visiting here. I had hoped the prayers would be as much of a blessing to her as they seemed to have been for him. Little did I know what a blessing they would be. Esther testified that the words that were prayed over Johnny *confirmed* all the prayers and words she was receiving in London and her parents were receiving in New Zealand. Isn't the Holy Spirit incredible? Don't we serve a faithful, supernatural, magnificent God! "From the Lord comes deliverance. May your blessing be on your people." (Psalm 3:8) "You turned my wailing into dancing; you removed my sackcloth and clothed me with joy, that my heart may sing to you and not be silent. O Lord my God, I will give you thanks forever." (Psalm 30:11-12)

Life-altering healing and deliverance took place in unison in three different locations around the globe. God is El Shaddai, the All-Sufficient One. We were seeing and hearing firsthand how His provision, mercy, and grace had been extended and received, and it was a day none of us will ever forget. "And God is able to make all grace abound to you, so that in all things at all times, having all that you need, you will abound in every good work." (2 Cor. 9:8) "Now to him who is able to do immeasurably more than all we ask or imagine, according to his power that is at work within us, *to him* be glory in the church and in Christ Jesus throughout all generations, for ever and ever! Amen." (Eph. 3:20-21) (Emphasis added.) Here, in her own words, is what Esther had to say about our time with her and the time after her visit with us in Charlotte:

> By the time Jonny and I came to Charlotte and I had the op-portunity to meet and share my story with the "Charlotte La-dies" as I call them, I was exhausted by the journey of infertility that Jonny and I had been on. But sharing my life story and testimony that day with the ladies, allowed for something really special to happen for me. It was like God provided this group of women to carry some of the burden for me. The feeling of loneliness I had felt lifted significantly.
>
> In the years that followed, God would continue to use this spe-cial connection with these women at key moments in our lives. There was one week in 2005 when I told Jonny that I was los-ing hope. That same day, I received an email from Anne saying that she had been praying specifically for us for the previous six weeks and she had a poem the Holy Spirit had given her that she felt prompted to send us. The title of the poem was "Hope."
>
> Then, in 2006, Anne and I started emailing one another much more frequently. As I would share my struggles, she would send words of encouragement and prayers that she or others in the group had felt prompted to speak over us. On October 1st of that year, Anne emailed a prayer asking God to bring me into a place of freedom, into a place of being able to receive all that God had for me. She ended by saying that she would keep us

in her prayers for the next eight weeks. On the 11th of November, 2006, after six years of infertility, I found out that I was pregnant! Our precious daughter Ruby was born in July of the following year. I still marvel at how God used a friendship and prayer on the other side of the world to be such a huge support to Jonny and me during those difficult years. We continue to treasure the friendships that began during that time.

To date, Jonny and Esther have had a second child, a son named Theo. I don't think any of the women who were at the meeting that day Esther shared her testimony will forget the reality of God's faithfulness, redemption, and renewal. All of us that day became more aware of the vastness of the Spirit's work, and the detail to which He allows us to participate when we yield to His leading and follow His path.

Setting the Stage

Though we wrapped our meetings up in November, there was already something brewing behind the scenes for the new year. Anjie and I traveled to Taylorsville, North Carolina to spend a morning with Alan Smith, asking for his wisdom and discernment on how to move forward with the meetings. Since he had agreed to oversee our group, we felt we should check in with him and seek his guidance and counsel. We obviously had had an amazing season of worship and incredible time learning about operating in the Holy Spirit. But was it time to branch into something new?

During our visit with Alan, he talked to me about a course for prayer ministry from trailblazers in the area of inner healing through the workings of the Holy Spirit: John and Paula Sandford. They had put together a curriculum called the Elijah House School of Prayer Ministry. "John and Paula Sandford are co-founders of Elijah House, an international ministry established in 1974 in response to the Lord's call 'to restore the hearts of the fathers to their children, and the hearts of the children to their fathers.' (Mal. 4: 5-6) They set out to do this by equipping saints with biblical tools that are founded upon the universal laws in the Word of God. They are well known for their teaching ministry and many books, the most popular being *The Transformation of the Inner Man*. By now thousands of students have graduated from their basic and advanced Elijah House equipping schools."[7]

I was not familiar with the school but Anjie was as she had already gone through the Basic 1 training the school offered. I then found out Alan's sister, Sally Reep, who we had met when Latha Ramesh Pandian visited, was one of several local women who were certified administrators of the Elijah House School of Prayer Ministry. Alan said he would call Sally as he was confident he could line up some of the ladies to administer the school to us. As we spent the morning talking about his suggestions, all three of us came into agreement that this seemed like the next move for the group. It was exciting to think that this opportunity might very well be able to take place right in the comfort of my own home.

Alan then shared a vision he had had with us. My recollection of the vision is this:

> "There was a boy, and he was flying a kite in the wind. The kite was high up in the air, but it was spinning around in circles because it did not have a tail. The boy's granddaddy came into the vision and began to teach the boy about the proper way to fly a kite. When the Granddaddy pulled the kite out of the sky, he got a Bible. He tore out many pages of the Bible and tied them on as a tail for the kite. The grandson then put the kite back into the wind, and as he pulled the tension on the string, the kite took off again in the wind, this time with a tail, and the tail kept the kite flying as it went higher and higher." This is my understanding of the interpretation Alan shared that day: "The kite is us, the individual. The wind is the Holy Spirit. The tail is the Word of God. When the Wind, the Holy Spirit, catches us, the kite, He causes us to go higher in the things of the Lord, higher in the Spirit. Unless we have a tail attached to us, the

Word of God, we will not be able to fly correctly. The Word is vital in keeping us stable. The string, which causes tension, also represents the tension we experience here on earth. Tension is not always fun to deal with, but it is the tension in the string that helps the kite fly higher. It is the tension we experience in our lives that causes us to go to the Father, causes us to go up, to meet with the Lord, and receive His help so we can move forward in our life."

Alan said he believed it was time for us to get in the Word for a season. We had had such an incredible time in the wind of the Spirit, it just seemed wise to now get grounded in the truth of God's Word. We sure didn't want to be a kite flying in the wind of the Spirit without the tail of the Word on us. John 4:23-24 says: "Yet a time is coming and has now come when the true worshippers will worship the Father in spirit and truth, for they are the kind of worshipers the Father seeks. God is spirit, and his worshipers must worship in spirit and in truth."

I really did not know or have any kind of idea about what this next season would involve or even look like, but the Lord did. It was time to switch gears and head in a new direction. It was time to get into the Word. "My son, pay attention to what I say; listen closely to my words. Do not let them out of your sight, keep them within your heart; for they are life to those who find them and health to a man's whole body." (Prov. 4:20-22)

Alan made a call to his sister Sally, who in turn contacted the other women to see if they would be free and interested in setting aside several months to facilitate the school for us. All of them agreed, and Anjie and I met them at a local restaurant to hash out the details. You can imagine my surprise when I found out that the lead administrator, Sharon Pittman, had been at my home the day John Scotland visited. As we were remembering that day, Sharon mentioned that she was the one John had spoken these words to: "ding dong, ding dong, special delivery, special delivery." Suddenly, we all understood the meaning and revelation of those words. God knew back then that He was going to have Sharon bring into my home with a very special delivery: the Elijah House School of Prayer Ministry. We laughed as we saw the interpretation of that prophetic word open up before us, and we marveled at God's precision and good humor. Sharon was to become an integral part of our group and our training. God had been behind the scenes on our behalf getting everything ready for us and now the time had come for the gift of that preparation time to come to life.

Al Hardy and Bruce Kissell

Before the Elijah House School began, we kicked off 2005 by hosting Al Hardy and Bruce Kissell for the first time. Both were from St. Mary's Church and the last group of people who were coming to town for monthly meetings for the decision process that was still under way about whether St. Mary's was to plant a church in Charlotte or not.

Bruce was a worship leader at St. Mary's, and Al had been their Youth Pastor but was currently in seminary. More than thirty women showed up that morning, many for the first time. Word was continuing to get out about the home meetings and it was exciting to see what God was doing as we gathered in His name. We spent quite a lot of time in worship that morning and allowed the Spirit to move freely as we worshipped together. It was beautiful.

It is marvelous having people in my den, week after week, singing contemporary worship songs with one another as our guest worship leaders come with their guitars and lead us. The blend of voices in such a close environment makes for beautiful music. I especially love it when we would sing a particular verse over and over with the guitar and then a cappella. Many times during these meetings, we would sing for thirty or forty minutes. Sometimes I did not want it to stop. For many of us, who were from denominational churches, the opportunity to worship in this way was rare. That is why our worship opportunities with Anjie and visiting worship leaders from other churches were so special.

After worship, Al encouraged us to share what we were seeing or sensing in the Spirit. As the floor opened up for everyone to share, women began sharing visions, words and Scripture each felt the Holy Spirit was giving them. One woman spoke these words: "Whosoever drinketh of the water that I shall give him shall never thirst; but the water that I shall give him shall be in him a well of water springing up into everlasting life." (John 4:14 KJV) Then another woman quoted Isaiah 41:18: "I will open rivers on the bare heights and springs in the midst of the valleys; I will make the wilderness a pool of water and the dry land fountains of water." (NASB) The words signified what God was doing in our meetings. It was like the Lord had uncapped a well for us in our meetings, a well of the flow of His Spirit. It was a lovely picture thinking of the Holy Spirit as streams of living water flowing through our meetings.

What was really interesting was that after this meeting, many visitors who came to spend a morning after this meeting would "see" in the Spirit an uncapped well of living water, and it was another sign to us that God was using this time of meetings to be a place of refreshing and healing. I was also reminded of the first words the Lord ever spoke to me back in 2000: "come to the free living and drink of it as often as you like." It was marvelous to see those words come to life again.

Over the years, I have found several other Scriptures to confirm God's word to me. Revelation 21:6 says: "It is done. I am the Alpha and the Omega, the Beginning and the End. To him who is thirsty I will give to drink without cost from the spring of the water of life." Isaiah 55:1 says: "Come, all you who are thirsty, come to the waters." In John 4:14, we read: "whoever drinks the water I [Jesus] give him will never thirst. Indeed, the water I give him will become in him a spring of water welling up to eternal life." In Jeremiah 2:13, the Lord calls Himself "the spring of living water." And lastly, in Revelation

7:17, Scripture says: "For the Lamb at the center of the throne will be their shepherd; he will lead them to springs of living water. And God will wipe away every tear from their eyes." Oh that everyone would dip into this gift of living water and enter into life in Jesus' name.

Al shared a little of his own personal testimony and then began his talk saying: "What I have learned is ultimately, Christianity is all about seeking more of God; and when we do that, we begin a relationship with Jesus and the way we do that is by His Spirit. Following the Spirit is what it's all about—it's one of the main things the church is created to do; and that is what I see is happening in this group. Encountering God is supposed to lie at the very heart of our experience of church."

Al then preached the rest of the morning from 1 Corinthians 14:1: "Follow the way of love and eagerly desire spiritual gifts, especially the gift of prophecy." He reminded us that when we eagerly desire the spiritual gifts, things begin to happen and people will begin to notice. That was already happening as we gathered each week. People were hearing about the meetings and taking notice and visiting. We are to also follow the way of love, he said, and as a group, we needed to make sure we modeled love, leaving love in our wake. Scripture says we should eagerly desire to prophecy. Again, the reason prophecy is *so* important in the church today is because it builds up and encourages the body of believers. Prophetic words are like streams of living water to the church when given by the Spirit and in love. Al encouraged us to put "listening to God" into practice. If you are not asking God what to do and not getting still to hear His voice, chances are you will eventually get off track. As we got still and listened to the Spirit, we began praying and prophesying words of life over one another. It was another awesome time in the Spirit. The new year was starting off on a solid word and heading in a wonderful direction.

I got an email from a woman who visited us during a meeting as the new year unfolded. I was once again reminded that these meetings were of the Lord. This is part of what she wrote: "Anne, I wanted to take a moment to thank you again for inviting me to come and for keeping me on your 'list.' Your home is a city of refuge. It is a place where people can gather and worship the Lord and receive His restoration. The difference between the gathering at your house in freedom to worship and receive the power of the Holy Spirit versus my weekly Bible study struck me today. Both are good and both are necessary but still very different. Because of my busy schedule, I almost did not come today. But I am so glad I came as I felt the Lord wanted me to. What a blessing to experience God's grace when we are obedient to His promptings."

Notes like this remind me that God's plan and purposes were unfolding and He was making an impact in the lives of everyone who came to spend time with Him. We had started a new year and had decided to move into a new direction for the next season of meetings. Up to this time, we had hosted over a dozen guest speakers from many parts of the world. Only God could have organized and orchestrated that. We were in the river of the Holy Spirit, flowing with Him and following His lead. The next adventure: The Elijah House School of Prayer Ministry. We were more than ready to move into deeper water and full of anticipation of what was to come.

Reflection

Hope was a key word for Esther and Jonny. It may be a word that you need to think about today. Do you find you have been in a situation for a long time and it just does not seem God is hearing or answering your prayers for help and change? Esther and Jonny felt that way. But God did answer them. The Lord is behind the scenes right now acting on your behalf. Sometimes we have to be patient and wait. Today, if you find yourself still struggling with unresolved issues or situations that are causing pain or confusion, tell the Lord about them again. And let us pray for your hope and trust muscle to be strengthened. He is faithful and He will see to completion the good work He has begun. "The plans of the Lord stand firm forever, the purposes of his heart through all generations." (Ps. 33:11)

Prayer

Heavenly Father, I call on the hope that You offer to me today; hope that will sustain me, hope that will anchor me, hope that will keep me in peace. You know what I am hoping for Lord. You know the desires of my heart. Thank You that You know my thoughts and hear my prayers for _____ (name the thing that you need hope for today). Holy Spirit, rise up in me and lead me to that place of rest and peace as I remember to trust You in all things, in Jesus' Name I pray. Amen.

Here is the poem I sent to Esther in 2005:

"Hope"

Hold onto hope; don't let it go. It's a lifeline, and it is secure

As you make your way down the trodden path, with hope your life will be restored.

Hang onto hope, praise God in the midst. His countenance and ways are sure

For when you hang on to the hope in the midst, your trial will be easy and pure.

Hold onto hope, He says in His word. And His peace, let it reign in your life

For His ways are just, His ways are not ours, but He knows the right place and right time.

Thank God for the hope. Thank God for His power. Thank God for His passion and grace

Thank God for His endless and wonderful love, His desire to sustain in the race.

And when you hold on to the hope that He gives, the power of the Spirit comes through

The battle seems less of a burden to bear for His hand is what's carrying you.

Praise God for the hope. Praise God for His plan. Praise Him and His Spirit and Son

With God as our hope, our dreams will come true. Victory—in the end will be won![8]

Suggested Bible Readings

Ecclesiastes11:5-6; Romans 12:12; Romans 15:13; Hebrews 6:13-19

CHAPTER 11

The Elijah House
School of Ministry

ANJIE AND I SHARED WITH the group Alan Smith's
suggested direction to take John and Paula Sandford's Elijah House
Basic 1 Prayer Ministry Training Course. When the women heard
about the meeting with Sharon Pittman, "the ding-dong lady," and
learned that she was going to be the lead administrator of the Elijah
House School, there was great excitement. We were seeing the prophetic words John Scotland had spoken over Sharon back in the fall
come to life, and we knew they had implications that would affect all
of us. Many of the women knew of the Sanfords' ministry and some
had read their books, so this next step seemed logical and right on
target.

We began getting the word out to those we thought might be

interested in participating. To my complete surprise, I received an email from a woman who was part of a prayer ministry team not associated with our group, and in the email, she "warned" me not to get involved with the Elijah House School, because she said it was not Scriptural. The email completely confused me and made me very uneasy. It was my understanding that the Elijah House School was totally based on Scripture. Then, others from our group began getting emails and phone calls from the same woman "begging" them not to attend the Elijah House School, as she suggested it was "demonic." I couldn't believe it. I thought, "Here we go again." When opposition comes, it is time to press in to the Lord in prayer. It can also be a sign that you are on the right track.

Warfare can come when the enemy does not want you to advance in your relationship with the Lord. This was not the first time opposition had come knocking. But this opposition was not just coming against me, it was coming against all of us. We all trusted Anjie and her endorsement of the Elijah House School, and we certainly trusted Alan Smith and his recommendation. We had come to know Alan to be a man of godly wisdom, honor, and integrity. He is not one to seek glory for himself, and the fruit of his ministry is clearly evident as is the fruit of the Sandfords' ministry. God had chosen Alan to oversee us and encourage us as we grew in our faith, and we knew he wanted only the best for us.

The Lord also knew our hearts' desire was to grow deeper in relationship with Him. He knew we did not want to enter into anything that was not of Him. So, we began to seek the Lord, trusting He would show us if this was something we were not suppose to get involved with. "Find rest, O my soul, in God alone; my hope comes from him. He alone is my rock and my salvation; he is my fortress, I will not be shaken. My salvation and my honor depend on God; he is my mighty rock, my refuge. Trust in him at all time, O people; pour out your hearts to him, for God is our refuge," (Ps. 62:5-8)

As I look back at my personal journals during this time, I can see that I was in constant prayer about hosting the Elijah House

School. I also had many dreams. In one dream, Anjie and I were in a comfy cozy bus traveling down a beautiful road with a lot of other women. We came to a place in the road where we could visibly see all four seasons displayed in their splendor. It was a sight to behold. In one quadrant was spring, in another, summer, in the third one was fall and in the fourth, winter. All of the women on the bus were really excited as we collectively chose to change directions and drive out of the summer season into the winter season. In the winter quadrant, the trees were magnificently covered in silver. The picture was calm, quiet, and serene. There was a dusting of snow on the road ahead and all around. As we looked behind, we saw the summer season fade. It was represented as a field of brilliantly colored flowers as tall as the car windows.

When I looked up the meaning of "winter" in one of my prophetic books, (see list in Resource section) I found it meant "the Word." Alan had made it clear we were to move into a season of the Word and that was why we all believed the timing of the Elijah House School was right. "Snow" in the prophetic can mean: pure, grace, covered, unrevealed, unfulfilled. This is what I wrote in my journal: "I think this dream is significant to the season we are about to enter into with the Elijah House School. I sense we are going to be looking into things in our lives that may be covered or unrevealed like sin, shame, hurts, pains, and unforgiveness. But with God's purity and grace, we are making the right decision to move into this new season so we can be made whole, and therefore walk out of it with newness of life and fullness of who it is we are in Jesus." I had no doubt that this dream was about this decision to host the Elijah House School and it gave me peace to know everyone on the bus was on board with the decision. "Commit your way to the Lord; trust in him and he will do this: He will make your righteousness shine like the dawn, and the justice of your cause like the noonday sun." (Pss. 37:5-6)

I also received many email devotions, one of which talked about not listening to the static but to tune my radio to the voice of the Father and move in the direction He is telling me to move in. Soon after

I received this word, a funny thing happened. Anjie and I headed off on a scheduled one-night retreat. I had invited her to be the speaker at our women's church retreat. When we woke up the next morning to head back home, we could not believe it when we looked outside and saw it was snowing! Although it was January, it was not predicted, so we were all caught by surprise. It was a beautiful sight and very similar to the picture of the winter scene in the dream I had had. We were near Valle Crucis and the winding road, beautiful fields, and trees were covered in a dusting of snow. As we were getting in our car to leave, Anjie pulled out a pair of ear plugs from her coat pocket and said this: "Anne, here are some ear plugs. I think these are for you. There are going be times coming up when you will need to just plug your ears to what others around you are saying." Well, I am not sure if that word was about all that was being stirred up around us regarding the Elijah House School or if it was a word for some future event, but I received that word as being from the Lord. We were to plug our ears to the static, and as a group, we chose not to listen to the opposition around us and we moved forward with our plans to attend the school. What a right decision it was for all of us; a right decision indeed.

Before we began the Elijah House School, I received an email from Al Hardy, who was in London at the time. This is some of what he wrote: "Anne, How's it going? You have been on my mind recently and I wanted to check how you were getting along. How is the prayer going, and is your women's group still meeting? Anne, God has His Hand on you. You are a pioneer, which isn't always easy, and I worry that you may not always receive the encouragement necessary to press on. If so, do let me know, as we are thinking of you and I would like to pray more for you in all you are doing."

I find myself getting a bit emotional reading this again. The timing of this email from Al was perfect as we were moving ahead with the Elijah House School. This is what it is like to be connected with someone in the Holy Spirit; God will use them to write a word of encouragement just at the right time. "Dearest friends, you were always so careful to follow my instructions when I was with you. And now that I am away you must be even more careful to put into action God's saving work in your lives, obeying God with deep reverence and fear. For God is working in you, giving you the desire to obey him and the power to do what pleases him." (Phil. 2:12-13 NLT)

The Elijah House organization granted us permission to host the school in my home, but there were specific guidelines and basic requirements that had to be followed and fulfilled to administer the school. There were applications and paper work to complete, and a schedule that needed to be worked out. The Elijah House School of Ministry Basic 1 course is a sixty-hour course that we were going to try and get through in thirteen weeks. There were videos to watch, small group sessions to participate in, and books to purchase and read. We were also required to be at every class. No misses allowed. This was a *huge* commitment and we continually prayed that only those who were supposed to attend would sign up. We were up to the challenge.

Sharon Pitman, the lead facilitator, came to review the schedule and talk to us about the school. It was decided we would meet every Tuesday from 9:00 to 1:30, but we also had to meet a couple of Thursdays in order to get the course completed. We had to meet within the boundaries of our children's school schedules, and we needed to have the course completed before our children got out of school in June.

Sharon spent some time explaining in more detail what the Elijah House School for Prayer Ministry Basic 1 training was all about. The purpose was to give Scriptural foundation for truth, allowing each one of us an opportunity to open our hearts to that Truth. The training we would receive would renew our minds and the results would be life transforming. Meeting together would also provide safety. There would be basic trust levels we would enter into with one another that would improve over time through the small group meetings. We had already begun that process as we had been meeting for a year now, but it sounded like we would be challenged to go even deeper in opening ourselves up to one another. The small groups would be vital to our own personal healing and growth, and they would offer opportunities for us to learn new ways to minister to one another in love and acceptance. She likened the school to a hardware store that would give us tools for our Spiritual tool belt: tools for ministry and tools to help us build relationships. She also said that the relationships we established from our time together would be gifts that would connect us for a lifetime.

Sharon introduced us to the other ladies who would be helping her administratively. Anna Carroll Mottershead, aka AC, Joyce Miller, and Mary Ann Stewart are three wonderful women of faith who selflessly gave their time to us. We came to grow in love and appreciation for them and all they did to help us through the course. There was excitement and anticipation in the air when we ended our meeting with Sharon. We were ready to commit and get started.

As we geared up for our start date in March, Alan came back to visit us again to give us a pep talk in hopes of encouraging us in our commitment. He reminded us that God is in the business of transforming us. "Of all the things I have touched, this one course is in a package that will bring together the strongest prophetic tools I have ever seen to help sharpen the prophetic vision of God's people. God can really use us when He is able to move us to the place we need to be," he said.

What a powerful statement. As I write it makes me think of 2 Corinthians 3:16-18, which says: "But whenever anyone turns to the Lord, the veil is taken away. Now the Lord is the Spirit, and where the Spirit of the Lord is, there is freedom. And we, who with unveiled faces all reflect the Lord's glory, are being transformed into his likeness with ever-increasing glory, which comes from the Lord, who is the Spirit."

That was what we were getting ready to experience. Real transformation. The veil of the things that were holding us back, whether it be pride or guilt or shame or hate or any of the other many things that keep any of us from walking in freedom—those veils were coming off in the name of Jesus, and we were going to grow in strength and wholeness. Though we had no clue what we were really getting into, the Lord did, and His blessing and provision was showered on us in new and mighty ways those next three months. We were about to embark on an adventure that would challenge many of us in our weakest places, and mature us and heal us in ways that would change us forever.

Nineteen women signed up to take the course and four women committed to be here every week to facilitate and oversee the class. The number nineteen in the prophetic means "faith." Don't you love it? On March 8, 2005, we gathered for our first day of school and for the next three months we immersed ourselves into study, prayer, ministry, and fellowship. It was an incredible time and the Lord's hand was on it. Week after week, we dove into the lesson plans, which centered on God's Word. There were many videos to watch, and each video would end with a prayer ministry session demonstrating how to minister to one another in love. We were also required to have nine small group meetings, and during those gathering times, we learned to let our guard down and began getting real with one another. We also practiced ministering to one another during those small group sessions and we continued to get more confident in hearing the Holy Spirit's voice as we ministered the way He led.

Elijah House School Curriculum

The Elijah House School curriculum was chock full of information. We learned about issues involving bitter root judgments, (judgments we carry that cause bitterness towards a person or situation when we feel we have been wronged), trust, forgiveness, repentance, and restitution. God's spiritual laws were opened up to us as we learned about the spiritual principles of honoring your mother and father, the truth and reality of reaping and sowing, and how the inner vows we make, ("I am not smart so I won't ever achieve anything great," or "I will never marry") have power over our lives that we can carry with us for a lifetime if we do not acknowledge them, renounce them, and cut ourselves free from them.

We learned about burden-bearing principles, spiritual rebellion, and the importance of healing relationships, not only with family members, but with those who are in authority as well. We had sessions on deliverance ministry, and began to experience deliverance and inner healing ourselves. We learned that there are right ways to express our emotions and wrong ways, and we saw the importance of really acknowledging what we may be in denial about. We looked at strongholds, (a stronghold is a mindset; it is what we think and believe to be right, and it can either line up with the Word of God, or deny God's truth) and we looked at how our mindsets can have a positive or negative effect in our lives and the lives of others. As the course came to a close, we learned about many common errors that can occur when ministering to others, like insisting someone repent and forgive when they are not ready, or automatically assuming a problem is caused by demonic influence.

There is an old saying that goes like this: "wounded people wound people and healed people heal people." We were learning what it looked like to be healed instead of wounded, hope-filled instead of helpless, free instead of living in bondage. This time, the Lord was not just giving me a mustard seed to plant by hosting the Elijah House School in my home, but I was beginning to see that all nineteen of us were mustard seeds ourselves. By saying, "Yes Lord, we are willing to be planted, watered, and pruned so you can make us grow," we allow Him to do amazing things in our lives. So God planted us in the fertile ground of the Elijah House School. He nurtured us and tended to us though the curriculum and through the administrators so we could grow and mature. With our trust in the Lord and the Lord's purposes for each one of us, those three months became months of supernatural transformation. I believe He grew *all* of us up into new more mature, lovely, life-giving trees.

Nancy Moore's Testimony

Each woman has her own testimony of how the Elijah House School of Ministry blessed her. Nancy Moore was one of the nineteen who attended the school. Here is her personal testimony.

The Elijah House Training was life changing for me. The most rewarding yet dreadful part was the small group time. We spent a lot of time watching videos, but I think it would have meant very little if we had not practiced what we were hearing in our small group. I did not know anyone in my small group, so it was difficult to share intimate details of my life with strangers. However I found myself sharing shame and guilt from my past that I had never even shared with my best friends. I loved watching the Holy Spirit work through each one of us as we prayed and listened and asked questions. Each member of the team played an integral part. It was important to share what you were hearing or seeing. And interestingly enough, we all had a piece of the puzzle. I had made an inner vow concerning my motherhood twenty-eight years previously. The breaking of this vow in my life changed my life dramatically. I was finally able to become a confident and an effective mother, while trusting God to work though my sin in a new and freeing way.

Also, I must mention that the Elijah House training taught me some new truths that I have found very enlightening. Our culture honors certain sins, such as perfectionism, performance, and taking responsibility for everything and everyone. I began to see that these actions were trying to be God and not trusting God.

The Elijah House School also emphasized the negative long term consequences of unforgiveness and judgment in our lives, making me much more aware of this in myself and others. Since this training, I have become more and more convinced that much of our sin and struggles begin with unforgiveness."

Graduation

On May 31, 2005, we met for the last Elijah House School class. Of course we ended that wonderful day with a celebratory pot-luck lunch. Our group does like to have a meal together. The women surprised me with several special gifts as a thank you for hosting the school in my home.

The first gift I received was a beautiful chalice and matching communion plate. These gifts had significant and very personal meanings to me. I had been taught that only ordained priests could administer the bread and the wine. This is contrary to what we learn in the Bible. "As you come to him, the living Stone—rejected by men but chosen by God and precious to him—you, also, like living stones, are being built into a spiritual house to be a holy priesthood, offering spiritual sacrifices acceptable to God through Jesus Christ. But you are a chosen people, a royal priesthood, a holy nation, a people belonging to God, that you may declare the praises of him who called you out of darkness into his wonderful light." (1 Pet. 2:4-5,9)

The "holy priesthood" mentioned in this passage is the body of believers. Once you become a believer, you become part of the royal priesthood and all that the priesthood offers. Nowhere in the Bible does it say that we as believers can't share the sacraments with one another. I wonder if sometimes man's ideas and protocols get in the way of the Spirit, and when man writes into law things that are not Scriptural, the whole body can be misled and miss out on the blessings God intends for us. Those gifts were a symbol that represented a breaking off of a false teaching I had believed in. They have been used many times since to bless the women who have come through the doors of my home to gather in the Lord's name. The Lord has been honored every time we've gathered to break bread with one another. I treasure the communal cup and plate the women gave me. They will always signify to me the truth about who I am in Christ Jesus.

The ladies also gave me a beautiful necklace made by Melissa that had the following words inscribed on it from Ezekiel 47:9: "where the river flows everything will live," symbolizing the Holy Spirit, the living water, which brought new life to me. Again, I remembered those first words I ever heard the Lord speak. Lastly, the women gave me a cool folk art piece in the shape of an angel. The women know I believe in angels and I love folk art so this was another unique gift just for me. I was a bit overwhelmed by it all and it made for a most memorable day.

The following Saturday, we planned a barbecue to celebrate again, this time with our husbands and with Alan and his wife, Frankie. Sabrina Polly, one of the women who had attended the Elijah House School, invited us all over for what a wonderful evening. Alan spent a little time speaking to the group, especially to the husbands, sharing with them what the Elijah House School was all about. He summed it up like this: "The Elijah House School teaches how we should all come into agreement with God in what He is doing. Christianity is relationship—learning how to be in relationship with God and with one another. Through the Elijah House School, these women learned it is profitable to come into agreement with Him."

Then Joyce, one of the administrators, read a poem she had written describing us as yellow rose buds that were being tended to by the Master Gardener. Peggy Johnson, another woman who attended the school, read a poem the Lord had given her titled, "Harris Road Laundromat." It was fun to hear her compare the school to a Laundromat saying: "Each week going to Anne's was like going to a Laundromat with a basket full of dirty clothes. Jesus became the washing machine for all of our soiled stained garments and the detergent used to wash our dirty clothes was Gain detergent." Peggy likened the blood Jesus shed to bleach that removes our stains, and went on to say that the washing and tumbling, rinse, and spin cycles of the school got rid of all our dirt and offenses. It was a perfect description of what we had just gone through. "The best part," she said, "is the huge clothesline out back. That's where we each hang our garments in the warmth of the sun (son)." It was a great synopsis of our time together.

Peggy ended by quoting the following Scripture: "But whatever was to my profit I now consider loss for the sake of Christ. What is more, I consider everything a loss compared to the surpassing greatness of knowing Christ Jesus my Lord, for whose sake I have lost all things. I consider them rubbish, that I may *gain* Christ and be found in him, not having a righteousness of my own that comes from the law, but that which is through faith in Christ—the righteousness that comes from God and is by faith." (Phil. 3:7-9) (Emphasis added.)

New Life Church

The next day, on Sunday, May 6, we all drove to Taylorsville, North Carolina to New Life Church where we gathered one last time to celebrate our accomplishment. It was a powerful morning with fantastic worship and a wonderful message from Alan.

After Alan's sermon, I was asked to get up and testify. God, in His detailed way, gave me a picture on the ride up to Taylorsville that morning that mirrored what Alan had talked about in his sermon, which had been from Isaiah 40:3-5 about the highway to holiness. I was able sum up our experience in the Elijah House School by sharing with everyone what I had seen driving to New Life Church that morning.

Traveling on Highway 77 to Taylorsville, I passed miles and miles of huge trees that had been cut down along the highway. They were strewn all over the side of the road. Debris was everywhere. The trees had been cut down to level the land so the highway could be widened. There were dump trucks all along the highway picking up trees and branches, and there were mulching machines operating too. I saw it as a prophetic picture.

Cutting down the trees to widen Highway 77 so wider lanes could be built for easier travel and easier access was like cutting down the stuff in our lives so that we would have wider and easier access to our Heavenly Father. Bitter root judgments, unforgiveness, and deep inner vows because of hurt were some of the "trees" many of us had to cut down along the highway of our hearts. Dealing with those things in our lives that had obstructed our access to God was not always easy. I think it might even be fair to say that for some of us, there were weeks when we felt like a lot of the trash and debris was littered everywhere. But God, in His faithfulness, brought in dump trucks to pick up the debris—those people who prayed for us, those books we read, and the Elijah House course all helped remove the debris in our lives. And then the Lord brought in His mulching machine, the Holy Spirit, which helped us get rid of the remaining debris from those cut down trees. The debris of hurts and pains and realities we each had to face in our lives was now turned into mulch, mulch that consisted of new life, new freedom, forgiveness, joy, and peace.

Through the Elijah House School, those trees not only got cut down, root system and all, but healing, wholeness and cleansing occurred as a result. The highways of our individual hearts began to be cleared, and as we began to have new access to God, we were also able to receive more of God's love in our lives. It was a cool picture and the Spirit gave me the right words to express it in a way that made it all come together.

When the time came for us to receive our graduation certificates, we were called up individually, and then paired off in twos. Alan laid hands on each pair of women and prayed over each of us commissioning us to go out and do the work the Lord has called us to. Many saw gold dust manifested during this prayer time on themselves and on their loved ones. It was like the Lord decided He too was going to give us a memorable gift to celebrate that day! I have heard of many other times when people have seen gold dust appear. It is a powerful thing to behold. It was an amazing ending to a remarkable weekend. The Lord was transforming our hearts, our spirits, and our souls from glory to glory, and we all had a sense we would never return to the place where we had begun and never be the same.

Wilderness Time

After the church service and commissioning, we all went to lunch. Alan joined us and I ended up sitting next to him. It was during our meal that he referred to our house meetings as a "Glory House." He also said that since we had been in a season in the Word, it was probably time to get back into a season of the Spirit again. I had a real clear sense that we were to move forward into another season of the Spirit, and I was also a very clear in knowing we were not to go back to things they way things had been before the Elijah House School began. I voiced my thoughts to Alan and he agreed. He said he would be happy to help us "hold" or wait until God showed us what our next step was. In the interim, we would continue to meet.

Waiting during a transition time can be like a wilderness time. That is not a bad thing. Proverbs 3:5-6 says: "Trust in the Lord with all your heart and lean not on your own understanding; in all your ways acknowledge him, and he will make your paths straight." I had complete confidence that the Lord would show us our next move. I think we all had come to an understanding that the Lord would show us the way; all we had to do was wait and watch and take His lead. Alan encouraged me that day and I had expectation in my heart for our next round of meetings. "God wants us all to walk in supernatural life," he said, so I left lunch that day ready for a shift into more of the supernatural and could not wait to see what that might look like. "Wait for the Lord; be strong and take heart and wait for the Lord." (Ps. 27:14)

Reflection

I wonder if there is something that has happened in your life that has caused you to have a bitter root judgment against someone? Has there been a time when someone has come against you in a way that caused you to begin to feel bitter towards them and judge them? When I think back on the woman who was against us taking the Elijah House School, I see how her actions towards us could invite us to judge her. It was important that we did not give in to judging her. Although she had a wrong understanding of what the school was all about, we know her to be a woman who loves the Lord and desires to know Him. Hebrews 12:14-15 says: "Make every effort to live in peace with all men and to be holy; without holiness no one will see the Lord. See to it that no one misses the grace of God and that no bitter root grows up to cause trouble and defile many." Ask the Lord to show you if you have any bitter root judgments against anyone. If you do, maybe today is the day to lay them down. Once you recognize them, all you have to do is confess them, repent, and offer forgiveness. The Lord can bring new life and restoration to you, and through your healing, you will see new life begin to grow and bloom in your relationships. Don't be held captive to negative habits, judgments, hurts, or attitudes. Let them go today in Jesus' Name and begin walking in new freedom and resurrected life.

Prayer against Bitter Roots from the Elijah House School Basic 1 workbook:

"Lord, I recognize I have judged _____ for _____ and have locked myself into that same behavior / attitude. I choose to forgive him / her for hurting me, and I choose to release my right to hold this offense against him / her, knowing it is up to You alone to judge all of us. Please forgive me for the sinful ways I have reacted and for the ways in which I have done the very same to others. (Be specific in naming those who have hurt you and those you've hurt. Be specific in naming any situations that are coming to mind as you pray now.)

"Lord Jesus, forgive me for judging _____. Now I am reaping the same patterns throughout my life. I choose to forgive, and release my anger and bitterness to You, Lord. Please remove it from my heart. Forgive me also for my part in tempting _____ to do the very thing I hated by the power of my bitter root expectancies and judgments."[9]

Thank You Lord for forgiving me. Thank You Lord for setting these bitter root attitudes, thoughts, and judgments at the foot of the cross in Jesus' Name. Holy Spirit, come. Fill me anew with Your presence and fill in the vacated areas now with Your love and Your light. Help me to walk in a new way, free from any bitter root thoughts, words, or deeds. I ask this in Jesus' Name. Amen.

Suggested Bible Readings

Galatians 6:6-14; 1 John 1:5-9

Other Books

Some of the Books we read during the Elijah House School are: *The Transformation of the Inner Man* by John and Paula Sandford; *Healing The Wounded Spirit* by John and Paul Sandford; *Restoring The Christian Family* by John and Paula Sandford, and *The Renewal of the Mind* by John L. Sandford and R. Loren Sandford.

Interpreting the Symbols and Types by Kevin J. Conner

Understanding the Dreams you Dream Volume 2 by Ira Milligan

CHAPTER 12

The Train Is Switching Tracks

AS I TRIED TO WRAP things up from the Elijah House School for a summer break, the doors at my home would not close. I started getting calls from folks who just wanted to stop by and talk. Next thing I knew, I would be ministering to them. Divine appointments were popping up everywhere. On top of that, the women did not want to quit meeting for the summer. So we made an effort to meet once a month.

We began calling ourselves the Glory Girls as a result of Alan Smith's word about us being a Glory House. It was crystal clear to me and everyone else that these meetings and gatherings in my home were being completely directed by God for His purposes. "This service that you perform is not only supplying the needs of God's people but is also overflowing in many expressions of thanks to God. Because of the service by which you have proved yourselves, men will praise God for the obedience that accompanies your confession of the gospel of Christ, and for your generosity in sharing with them and with everyone else." (2 Cor. 9:12-13) It seemed He was nowhere near ready to call it a wrap. It was also becoming clearer that my role was shifting as the meetings continued. When Sharon Pittman arrived on the scene to facilitate the Elijah House School, the leadership role naturally switched from Anjie to Sharon. Anjie had really been leading the group up to that point when other speakers were not visiting. Looking back on it now, I can see that this shift in leadership was a purposeful one as the Lord had plans to move the group into a new dimension and new direction. And after the Elijah House School, I began taking on more of a leadership role. I began to feel more confident in hearing God's voice and following His lead for the group, and I was also being encouraged by many of the women to step up into this new position.

There was a real stirring happening among the women at this time. We had been catapulted into a higher place in the Spirit as a result of the Elijah House School, and we just could not get enough of the Lord. We were all in agreement we did not want it to be "business as usual."

The Lord placed several Scripture verses across our paths during the summer months that encouraged us and confirmed to us that we were on the right path. God's Word serves as a beacon of light. When we follow His light, we are sure to be on the right path. "Your Word is a lamp to my feet and a light for my path. Your statutes are my heritage forever; they are the joy of my heart. My heart is set on keeping your decrees to the very end." (Ps. 119:105, 111-112)

In September 2005, I had a very clear vision. In the vision, I saw a train on a train track. The lever that was used to switch the train from one track to another moved, and the train began to head down a new track heading in a new direction. "The train is switching tracks," I wrote in my journal and the reality of that vision was soon to come.

Al Hardy and Ed Flint

During this time we heard that St Mary's had decided to plant a church in Charlotte, and Al Hardy and his wife Niki had been called to Pastor the church. We were thrilled. We had grown very fond of the folks from St. Mary's, as they had played an integral part in sharing the Gospel and the life of the Holy Spirit with us. When I found out Al was going to be back in town for a visit, I invited him to come again to spend a morning with our group. I was excited to see Al and hear all about what was getting ready to happen. With him was a fellow named Ed Flint. Ed was another worship leader at St. Mary's. He led us in a time of worship before Al shared a message with us.

Al opened the morning by reading Psalm 130, which says: "Out of the depths I cry to you, O Lord; O Lord, hear my voice. Let your ears be attentive to my cry for mercy. If you, O Lord, kept a record of sins, O Lord, who could stand? But with you there is forgiveness; therefore you are feared. I wait for the Lord, my soul waits, and in his word I put my hope. My soul waits for the Lord more than watchmen wait for the morning, more than watchmen wait for the morning. O Israel, put your hope in the Lord, for with the Lord is unfailing love and with him is full redemption. He himself will redeem Israel from all their sins."

He continued: "When we are in a waiting period, the uncertainty in the waiting can cause difficulty within our being. Sometimes, we agonize over the waiting because we don't know or understand what we are waiting for. We are so used to living in this 'get it quick' world and mentality, waiting can sometimes become very uncomfortable. There might even be the tendency to try and make things happen, which can result in a sinful or negative reaction."

We know the Bible is full of those kinds of stories, such as the story about Abraham and Sarah. The Lord promised them that they would have children as numerous as the stars, but things were taking much longer than they had expected. Ten years passed and still no children. (Gen. 15) Those who know the story know that Abraham ends up sleeping with Hagar, Sarah's maidservant. Their inability to wait on God's timing did not derail God's promise, but it did wreak some havoc and added a whole new dimension to what God has intended.

Al suggested that when God invites us to wait, it is not to be an empty, hollow time. It can be a really blessed time. We can wait knowing that God keeps His promises and sees to completion the good work He has begun. "In all my prayers for all of you, I always pray with joy because of your partnership in the gospel from the first day until now, being confident of this, that he who began a good work in you will carry it on to completion until the day of Christ Jesus." (Phil. 1:4-6) God's Promises are True. "But do not forget this one thing, dear friends: With the Lord a day is like a thousand years, and a thousand years are like a day. The Lord is not slow in keeping his promise, as some understand slowness. He is patient with you, not wanting anyone to perish, but everyone to come to repentance." (2 Pet. 3:8-9)

Al went on to say that the other amazing thing about waiting is that when we are in a waiting time, we are not alone. He is always with us. "The Lord your God goes with you; he will never leave you nor forsake you." (Deut. 31:6) He is there, waiting for us to invite Him into our waiting.

Isn't that awesome! God's deepest desire is to walk with us in our journey. So in the pain, the anxiety, the restlessness and at times, the agony of waiting, God is waiting there, challenging us to turn from the natural reaction and accept His rest—rest that can only be found in God's unfailing love. It's not always easy to wait but we know that God will meet us there, and bless us in the process with His presence.

Al's word for the Glory Girls that day was right on target. Thank You Lord. After his talk, we spent time being still and waiting on the Lord. Suffice to say, it was another powerful morning in the Spirit with one another. "I wait for the Lord, my soul waits, and in his word I put my hope." (Ps. 130:5)

Transition Time

Seasons change in nature, and they change in the Spirit as well. You cannot get too comfortable where you are in the Spirit for too long or you risk missing out on the next thing the Lord has in store for you. The time had come for the train to switch tracks and as I knew from experience, the switch may not be easy.

In this midst of this time of waiting and transition, I made a mistake that caused some problems. Anjie, Alan, and I met one evening to talk about it, and we also talked about the changes that were occurring in the group, especially the changes that were occurring in the leadership role. Alan reviewed a Biblical principle from Matthew 18. Verses 15-17 talk about the importance of going to your brother (or sister) first to talk to them if there is something that needs to be discussed instead of going to others first. "If your brother sins against you, go and show him his fault, just between the two of you. If he listens to you, you have won your brother over. But if he will not listen, take one or two others along, so that 'every matter may be established by the testimony of two or three witnesses.' If he refuses to listen to them, tell it to the church; and if he refuses to listen even to the church, treat him as you would a pagan or a tax collector."

There had been an incident with Anjie, and instead of continuing a conversation with her directly, I first sought the advice of one of the other women in the prayer group. When Anjie found out, her feelings were hurt. Alan brought us all together to clear the air. I apologized to Anjie and I accepted Alan's correction in this.

It was a tense time. The Lord was shifting all of us, and as I have said before, change is not always easy or comfortable. Anjie and Alan, in agreement, decided that it was time to "release" Anjie from her leadership responsibilities to the group so she could move into the next thing God had for her and we as a group could move into the next thing God had in store for us. We decided on a date in October to be her last day. Alan also agreed to continue to oversee our group, which was a huge blessing. Switching tracks was harder than it had been before. Our group had deep love and appreciation for Anjie and we were going to miss her. It was another time of letting go of a secure and familiar way of doing things.

In the weeks that followed, we hosted two more guests. First we invited Sharon Pittman to visit. She agreed and spent a morning with us. She wanted to follow up with us as to how we were doing after the Elijah House School and she wanted to encourage us, as she was aware we were in a transition time as a group.

Sharon talked to us about what change and transition looks like, likening it to an inlet of water. "An inlet of transition has shallow waters and then they can get very narrow. When transition occurs, it's like you are in a bay and the waters are shallow and you are getting into this very narrow spot where God is ready to do something new and different. It's a place where sharks can pop up. The narrow, shallow water can be places where attitudes, problems, and difficulties with people arise. All of these things are forces that can come against us to try and keep us from transitioning and changing into that new place. She also said change and transition can represent new birth.

Sharon suggested that times of change and transition are processes we have to go through to enter into new, deeper, and more intimate places with the Lord, and it is in that new intimacy that we can experience more of God's agape love. "God comes to us in these narrow places of transition and birthing, to revive, renew, and ensure that we become vessels of His character." Sharon reminded us that we are to seek and be motivated by the love of God, and not the approval of others. "That means choosing to be obedient to the Lord over everything else. There are times when He will put us in a silence mode and we can't even speak of what is really going on, not even to the situation we have been in and functioned in and thrived in; He may just completely pull us out of that situation for a purpose to do a higher work, a much higher work, and there will not be a man that can understand. But," she assured us, "when we are in that process of change, it is for His ultimate glory. Ministering out of God's love is what it is all about."

I must admit her words came at just the right moment for me. I can't stand any kind of conflict with girlfriends, and the situation with Anjie had been painful to both of us. I heard Sharon's message clearly that day and felt the Lord speaking directly to me. As a woman who has given birth twice, I know transition is the most difficult part when delivering a baby, and this transition time was harder than any other I had been involved with to date.

"Therefore, as God's chosen people, holy and dearly loved, clothe yourselves with compassion, kindness, humility, gentleness and patience. Bear with each other and forgive whatever grievances you may have against one another. Forgive as the Lord forgave you. And over all these virtues put on love, which binds them together in perfect unity. Let the peace of Christ rule in your hearts, since as members of one body you were called to peace." (Col. 3:12-15)

Sabrina Colston

The very next week, Sabrina Colston from Flames of Fire Ministry came to be our guest. Sabrina was excited to be with us and was full of energy. Once we were all gathered, she immediately began preaching and referred us to a passage in Matthew 7:16: "By their fruit you will recognize them." Isn't God something? The Lord will send people over and over again to make sure you get the truth He wants to impart.

Sabrina said that as we enter into relationship with other people and other ministries, it will be important for us and for those we have relationships with to operate not only in the gifts of the Spirit but also in the fruits of the Spirit. "But the fruit of the [Holy] Spirit [the work which His presence within accomplishes] is love, joy, (gladness) peace, patience (an even temper, forbearance), kindness, goodness (be-nevolence), faithfulness, gentleness (meekness, humility), self-control (self-restraint, continence). Against such things there is no law [that can bring a charge]." (Gal.5:22-23 AMP). Understanding this truth, "by their fruit you will recognize them," Sabrina suggested you will not be deceived. The enemy can imitate the gifts, she said, but he can-not imitate the fruits. Watching to see if the fruits are being displayed in a person or ministry will help you in discerning if something or someone or some ministry is of the Lord or not.

Sabrina said that we have to recognize that we all have different personalities, different ways of ministering, and different ways we see things; we are different members of the same body. "Just as each of us has one body with many members, and these members do not all have the same function, so in Christ we who are many form one body, and each member belongs to all the others." (Romans 12:4-5) "In those differences," Sabrina said, "there will be times when we won't get along with each other or agree with what or how something should be done. There may be times we get frustrated with one another. That's OK. That's normal. What we *do* have to remember is to communicate with one another. Communication is key."

Sabrina then had us turn to Matthew 18. Sound familiar? Verse 15 says: "If your brother sins against you, go and show him his fault, just between the two of you." Maybe this was a lesson all of us need-ed to learn. Alan had talked to me about this with Anjie, and now Sabrina was getting this message out to the group. "We need to be grown-ups when these differences pop up," she said. "We need to ad-dress the issues with one another, shake off the offenses and move on. The enemy wants us to focus on the negative things. God wants us to look at the big picture and operate with one another in the fruits of the Spirit. We sure don't want to miss what opportunities God has for us, but we will miss them when we allow ourselves to get caught up in some petty thing that entangles us."

I am reminded now of the word John Scotland shared with us a year earlier about offense. Offense is a tool the devil uses to derail

God's people and His agenda. I think we can easily pick this tool of offense up, not realizing the harm it can cause us or those around us. May we all be ever mindful of this tactic of the enemy, and may we be wise not to fall prey to offense as we mature and walk in the ways of the Lord.

Sabrina continued: "As women, we sometimes tend to be more emotional about things and can get our feelings hurt easily. It is not always easy to walk in the fruits, but the more mature we become in Christ, the more our old nature dies and our new nature comes to life. As a result, the more the fruits will be evident in our lives."

Sabrina also likened it to another Scripture truth: "In the way we have to have the Spirit and the Word together, we have to have the gifts and the fruit together. In order to fly in balance," she said, "you will always want to see the fruits with the gifts." Philippians 2:12-15 says: "Continue to work out your salvation with fear and trembling, for it is God who works in you to will and to act according to his good purpose. Do everything without complaining or arguing, so that you may become blameless and pure, children of God without fault in a crooked and depraved generation."

The rest of the morning was spent talking about the gift of intercession. Sabrina described intercession as an opportunity for us to co-labor with the Lord. The Holy Spirit gives us the prayers to pray, the prayers then go back to Jesus, the great intercessor. Jesus is then able to release from heaven that which needs to happen on earth. "Christ Jesus, who died—more than that, who was raised to life—is at the right hand of God and is also interceding for us." (Rom. 8:34)

Sabrina referred us to a passage in Exodus 32 to use Moses as an example for us to follow as we grow in the gift of intercession. In the story, Moses is on the mountaintop with the Lord, and the Israelites below get antsy waiting for him to return. They go to Aaron and complain. And then they take matters into their own hands. Instead of being patient, they build a golden calf and begin worshipping it. God sees what is happening and gets very angry, angry enough to want to wipe the people out. But Moses comes to their defense. He interceded and, "sought the favor of the Lord." (Exod. 32:11) "Then the Lord relented and did not bring on his people the disaster he has threatened." (Exod. 32:14)

Now there were some consequences to this behavior by the Israelites. The Bible tells us about three thousand died as a result of this rebellion. But Moses, with his heart in the right place, went back to the Lord to make atonement for their sin. That word "atonement" is key to understanding where Moses' heart was. Moses desired to reconcile God and the Israelites, and he asked the Lord to "please forgive their sin—but if not, then blot me out of the book you have written." (Exod. 32:32). Moses had such a heart for the people he was interceding for that he said to God, if you don't forgive them, then you can't forgive me either. Moses did not accuse. Instead, he stood in the gap on their behalf and interceded for them, going before the Lord and asking for forgiveness. Sabrina challenged us with a question: "Are you willing have a heart like Moses for the people you pray for? Are you willing to have a heart like Moses for the leaders in this nation? Are you willing to have a heart like Moses for the leaders in your churches? Are you willing?"

You could have heard a pin drop. The room was so quiet. What a convicting question. I think it is one we should always keep in our minds as we are called by the Lord to intercede for someone or something. We should have a heart like Moses.

The morning ended with Sabrina prophesying over the group, praying and laying hands on each of us. It was a powerful prayer and I am ending this chapter with a few of the things she said over us. I hope that maybe her words can come full circle and bless *you* now as you read them out loud today. I say to you it is time to step up and move out into what the Lord is calling you to. Just do it. The time has come.

Sabrina's prayer:

"Thank You Lord that I am rising up, rising up and taking my position and taking my stand and it is You Lord, You Lord, You

Lord and nobody, nobody, nothing, no way, no how can argue against You Lord, can argue against Your purposes! Hallelujah! Let Your fire, fire, fire, burn, burn, burn.

Stop waiting for somebody to confirm it.

Stop waiting for somebody to tell it to you again.

You've been told it enough so now go with it. It is time to take the chance."

Then she said, "I feel there is a little expectancy of 'this is going to be the word that is going to set me out. She's going to give me the word that suddenly is going to break though the dam and I'm gone.' But I heard the Lord say, 'you tell them the dam has already been broken. You don't have to wait for another prophetic word or prayer over you.' *It's already done!* So start walking in it and He will give you more. Walk in what you have and He will give you more. So you don't need any more confirmation. You don't need any more. You're OK. It's just like the Nike phrase, 'Just do it!' Just do it ladies, just do it! You don't need anything else. You've been confirmed. You've been sealed. You've been blessed. You've been given. You have favor. All those things are already yours. Amen. Do you believe? Amen."

I have to tell you, I have such a witness in my spirit reading these life-giving words again. What a timely word for me as I now write my first book. I have learned prophetic words have many layers of revelation, and they seem to come round and round again to bless and encourage. I am stunned at the timing of reading these words again. And I am once again in complete awe of God's orchestration of this entire season the Glory Girls had just been through.

You may remember the first speaker we ever hosted from St. Mary's was Nick Herbert. Nick, on numerous occasions, referred to the Nike slogan, *"Just do it."* Now, as the Lord was transitioning our group out of one season and into another, He ended the season with the same words He started it with: *"Just do it!"* I don't know about you, but this blesses me and it surprises me, and it puts me in a place of reverence and wonder as I see the detail to which God the Father, Creator, Provider, and Sustainer has gone to in order to bless a group of women in Charlotte, North Carolina who chose to meet with Him week after week to fellowship in His name and to get to know Him better.

This gathering was Anjie's last official meeting with us as a leader of the group. She did come back and visit us many times as we continued to meet, but she too was being called into a new season. Anjie ended up going to school and earning her teacher's certificate. She is now an elementary school teacher specializing in ESL. She still leads worship at conferences, at her church, and at other venues. God has been faithful to her and to us as a group, and she still is and always will be connected to us and counted as a Glory Girl.

"For this reason I kneel before the Father, from whom his whole family in heaven and on earth derives its name. I pray that out of his glorious riches he may strengthen you with power through his Spirit in your inner being, so that Christ may dwell in your hearts through faith. And I pray that you, being rooted and established in love, may have power, together with all the saints, to grasp how wide and long and high and deep is the love of Christ, and to know this love that surpasses knowledge—that you may be filled to the measure of all the fullness of God. Now to Him who is able to do immeasurably more than all we ask or imagine, according to his power that is at work within us, to him be glory in the church and in Christ Jesus throughout all generations, for ever and ever, Amen." (Eph. 3:14-21)

Reflection

When was the last time you found yourself waiting? When was the last time you found yourself in a time of change or transition? Maybe you are waiting for a child to find their way. Maybe you are waiting for a job opportunity. It could be you are waiting for a boyfriend or maybe you are waiting for that marriage proposal. Maybe there has been an untimely death in your family and you are just waiting for something, not really knowing what. Meet God in the waiting. He wants to be with you during this difficult and trying time. Trust Him to provide what you need during this time of waiting, and lean on Him. That is what He desires. Lean on Him, and let Him comfort you in the waiting.

Prayer

Father God, I know there are times we have to wait. Waiting is not always easy. I confess to You today, that I am struggling in the waiting. I need to know Lord that You are with me in this time of waiting. I specifically need patience as I wait for _____(name it out loud). Come Holy Spirit. Fill me afresh with Your presence. Fill me with the fruits of Your Spirit. May Your peace, that passes all understanding, guard my heart and mind today as I wait. I know You desire the very best for me. I know Your ways are different than mine. Help me to believe in hope and rest in the waiting, knowing everything that is meant to come to pass will. I ask this in Jesus' Name.

Suggested Bible Readings

2 Corinthians 1:3-7; Psalm 23, Psalm 27:14

CHAPTER 13

On Our Own

ON OCTOBER 11, 2005, THE Glory Girls gathered in my home for the first time in almost two years without a plan or a person to teach, preach, or lead us in worship. Up to this point, our time together had been a concentrated time of teaching and equipping. Now, the scene was shifting. It was just us and the Lord. I guess I can liken it to the first day a baby bird gets pushed out of the nest. It was time for us to fly on our own and we were excited.

Close to seventy women had walked through my front door to join in the meetings over the last twenty-two months. Some came for a certain period of time and some visited only once, but everyone had been blessed. By now, a smaller core group had formed, and this core group of twelve to fifteen women still wanted to meet. So for the remainder of the year, we continued to gather each week to be together and hang out with the Lord.

These last weeks before the holidays were spent time together in God's word, sharing dreams and visions, and ministering to one another as needs arose. We also had the opportunity to host John Scotland again. It was during this visit with John that we were introduced to the music of a worship leader based out of Lincoln, England. His name was Godfrey Birtill, and his music captivated us, ministered to us, and blessed us. Little did we know that one day, we would get to meet him and host him. I'll get to that shortly.

I would like to give you an idea of what our time together began looking like during this next season of meetings. Below are notes from a meeting we had the end of 2005. You will see that during our time together, we prayed, shared thoughts and words, read Scripture, discussed what we were seeing and hearing, and then we would pray again. Now that we were on our own, each meeting was unique to itself. No two were ever alike. This time in the life of our group was like a weekly treasure hunt. We never knew what the journey would look like, but we knew the Lord had treasure for us to find each week. We had the freedom to explore and express ourselves with one another. In this example, God confirmed to us that we were family. It's incredibly fun unearthing new revelations with sisters and brothers in Christ as the Spirit leads the way, and this is the way our meetings progressed for the next year when we did not have a planned teaching or a guest we were hosting.

Notes from Meeting, December 6, 2005

The meeting opened with corporate prayer, (meaning everyone was free to pray out loud and openly). We were declaring that when we take the time out of our schedules to meet with God, He *always* shows up. Revelation was expected and we knew we would have the eyes to see it. We prayed the Lord would take us to another level. We continued in intercession for a while and then got quiet.

Eventually I was led to pray over everyone, laying hands on each one, praying that the Lord would blanket everyone and their families with Peace.

Sharon L. then prayed Joy over everyone individually. We sang the song, "I've Got the Joy In My Heart."

Adrienne read 1 John 3:1: "How great is the love the Father has lavished on us, that we should be called children of God! And that is what we are! The reason the world does not know us is that it did not know him."

Sandra shared that she'd woken up with a burden to pray for the desire to be part of a family and have family relationship, and felt that the Lord had put that prayer on her heart. "Family equals blood relationship. That is what we are experiencing here as we meet on Tuesdays. We've prayed a prayer about *Peace*, and prayed a prayer about *Joy*, but the missing ingredient is *Love*. Growing in the Lord makes us grow in desire to relationship with one another." Then Sandra talked about the Glory. "It is our heritage to see the glory and it will be seen in all the world."

Sharon L. brought up a Ras Robinson email devotion that talked about putting on new robes. Sharon felt the Lord was showing her that the "new robe" Ras was referring to, was a *robe of relationship*. "God is calling us to be accountable and to be family. We have become a safe place to learn about what godly relationships with one another looks like."

As people shared how they have been hurt different times and places in their lives, they also shared the desire to have relationships with others.

Sandra said, "Aren't we tired of talking about how hurt we have been by other people or by the churches we attend? Aren't we tired of blaming others for our hurt and pain? It's time to take responsibility for ourselves. So what if you have a problem? *Let's be family.*"

Peggy then said, "We can lie down, prostrate on the floor and say, "Lord, we are desperate for you." Peggy then prayed for the Holy

Spirit to come right down into the center of us.

Intercession began again: "Lord, come on down and give us what *You desire for us*. You know what we need. Our prayers can be a public declaration for the Church as a whole. Let our faith, Lord, be greater than what it is we see." "Blessed are those who have not seen and yet have believed." (John 20:29)

Peggy continued: "God is the Head. We are representing the heart of Christ, and when our hearts are stirred, it is really *His* heart that is being stirred—the stirring is coming from God, who is the Head. The stirring is His desire. We have sort of a fuzzy feeling of His presence—*He wants **us more** than we can ever want Him!* He wants us to have more and it's time we yield to what He is saying to our hearts."

Then we prayed: "Lord, please change our hearts." The Lord has been working on our hearts.

I wondered out loud to the group if it might be a prophetic sign that the skin over my heart was being treated so new cells can grow. (Pre-cancerous cells had been detected on *my* décolleté and a topical chemo was burning away the old precancerous cells to make way for new, healthy cells to grow.)

Then Connie began talking about reproduction and how it is connected to the head.

"Think about reproduction—it's all in the hypothalamus. It's in the brain. The brain is in the head. Even the conception of children has got to come from God—the Head. Everything has to be signaled and motivated through the hypothalamus, which is the brain of every organ in the body."

Libby: "The hypothalamus is where the stimulating chemicals come from that stimulate the ovaries and the testicles to produce the reproductive hormones that are necessary and allow for conception to take place—even for the egg and sperm to be stimulated. All are stimulated by the hypothalamus."

Linda: "I am struck by the power the mind exercises over our bodies and our lives—that the very act of conceiving new life has to be initiated and authorized by the mind / brain. And throughout the whole cycle of this new life, the mind / brain continues to affect the progress of the pregnancy. Hence, it appears to me that the mind / brain must continue to cooperate, be in agreement with, the process and fully endorse (fully believe in) what is unfolding, although the end result has not yet materialized… it's believing without seeing. (John 20:29)

Linda continued: "The mind expects / assumes that this delicate process will indeed have a resolution. So then let's think of the mind—when we come to Christ, our mind is transformed. With our *transformed* mind, we give control to God to initiate and lead us; we put our belief in Him that He is at work in the situation and He will bring resolution to what we cannot yet see. We cooperate with what He had begun, obeying and also asking that He search our hearts and correct us through and through."

Peggy: "Talk about being a lump of clay and to be in His hands." Then Peggy prayed that everyone would be a lump of clay in God's hands and that God would mold us.

The words to a worship song came to my mind and I led us in song: "Take my heart and form it; Take my mind, transform us; Take my will, conform it, to Yours, to Yours, to Yours."[10]

We began to pray again, thanking God that He was the head of the church. We prayed for different churches in the area, and the need for new birth to come forth in them.

Margaretta: "Here's another thing. There have been a lot of kidney and urinary problems lately in my family. Kidney malfunctions—Pearl, our dog. She's at the end of her life, and the issue is over her urinating. I have wondered if this was a sign I needed to understand."

Connie: "It's the impurities. The kidneys take the blood, separate the blood, and cleanse out the blood and the impurities. Excretions are what come out of the body. This is about purification. It's about repentance again. It *is* a sign. It's the cleansing of the Spirit."

Christie: "Talk about trusting one another. Look at Jeremiah 17 in the Amplified.

'Thus says the Lord: Cursed [with great evil] is the strong man who trusts in and relies on frail man, making weak [human] flesh his arm, and whose mind and heart turn aside from the Lord. For he shall be like a shrub or a person naked and destitute in the desert; and he shall not see any good come, but shall dwell in the parched places in the wilderness, in an uninhabited salt land. *[Most] blessed is the man who believes in, trusts in, and relies on the Lord, and whose hope and confidence the Lord is.* For he shall be like a tree planted by the waters that spreads out its roots by the river; and it shall not see and fear when heat comes; but its leaf shall be green. It shall not be anxious and full of care in the year of drought, nor shall it cease yielding fruit.' (Jer. 17:5-8.) (Emphasis added.) Trust God! When you do that, you can't help but reproduce!

Now go to Ephesians 3:14-19: 'For this reason [seeing the greatness of this plan by which you are built together in Christ], I bow my knees before the Father of our Lord Jesus Christ, for Whom every *family* in heaven and on earth is named [that Father from Whom all fatherhood takes its title and derives its name]. May He grant you out of the rich treasury of His glory to be strengthened and reinforced with mighty power in the inner man by the [Holy] Spirit [Himself indwelling your innermost being and personality]. May Christ through your faith [actually] dwell (settle down, abide, make His permanent home) *in your hearts!* May you be rooted deep in love and founded securely on love, that you may have the power and be strong to apprehend and grasp with all the saints [God's devoted people, the experience of that love] what is the breadth and length and height and depth [of it]; [That you may really come] to know [practically, through experience for yourselves] the love of Christ, which far surpasses mere knowledge [without experience]; that you may be filled [through all your being] unto all the fullness of God [may have the richest measure of the divine Presence, and become a body wholly filled and flooded with God Himself!'" (Emphasis added.)

Christie went on to say; "If there is a separation between those who trust flesh and those who trust God, there is a collection of the ones who trust God. It is the body of Christ, who is presented without spot or wrinkle. And what is interesting in this Ephesians prayer is that the knowledge of the length, height, depth, and breadth of the love of God. You have to come with all the saints. It's *in relationships. It's under the Father for who every family in heaven and on earth is named,* so that by being in this living daily conversational relationship and embrace… there are times it is just Him and me, and that is so sweet, but to get a hold of the depth, length, height, and breadth, *we need each other* because the prayer is that you would have the power and be strong. It is not for the faint at heart. This is the risk because you have to trust God; but if you are not rooted in love and founded in love, you can't love one another. To be able to walk in Anne's house, take your shoes off, lay on the floor, open the refrigerator, stay overnight—*that's family!* And eventually, offense goes away, the judgments go away, and the expectations go away."

Lisa: "Can someone tie this up for me to understand?"

Sharon L.: "In John 17, Jesus says that they might be as one as we (the Father and the Son) are one. That's our heart today. Lord, we want to be unified in the depth, length, height, and breadth as one. John 17:20-21 says: "My prayer is not for them alone. I pray also for those who will believe in me though their message, that all of them may be one, Father, just as you are in me and I am in you. May they also be in us so that the world may believe that you have sent me.""

Connie: "The Lord has been showing us, for those who don't join us regularly, that we are a safe house for His presence. As we've been meeting, we've gotten to a place where we can be open and honest with one another. It is how we relate to one another. So when someone doesn't get it, there's a freedom to speak up because we are learning to flow in the Spirit together and how to keep ourselves in sync. We've got to be able to stop and question. If we don't, then the enemy can get in and steal the seed or understanding. We are getting real with one another. What we think being one means—we've got to let that die. It's you and me and God, you and me and God saying we are all one. "Just as each of us has one body with many members, and these members do not all have the same function, so in Christ we who are many form one body, and each member belongs to all the others." (Rom. 12:4-5)

Christie: "There is no need to have disunity. If *anyone* feels they don't have clarity like the Word of God says in Jeremiah 17, then ask. Hey! That's it! Jeremiah 17 is the old (verses 5-6). John 17 is the new! (Verses 7-8) Get it? Get it? Wow!"

Margaretta: "One of my prayers has been that I would be that tree by the river that would bear fruit that Christie read about in Jeremiah 17:8. When Christie was reading from the Amplified, it really lined up with my prayers and the whole topic of trust that I am going to talk about at the ECW (Episcopal Church Women) luncheon tomorrow. As *family*, we are peacemakers rooted in love. We don't want anyone leaving here today feeling like they don't belong."

Peggy shared her desire to be quiet, and we have a time of silence and quiet prayer. After a time of quiet, we began praying for the needs of some of the women and we ended the meeting.

The Fruit

The next day, I received an email from a woman who would visit our meetings on occasion and had visited this particular meeting day. She copied me in on an email she was sending to a Pastor who was also hosting weekly meetings at a church. Here is some of what she wrote:

"I am overjoyed to report to you that God is still in the business of recreating that which He first established in Acts: house meetings, with Jesus at the center, and believers coming together in Him through true and abiding relationship with one another. I have the impression that the meeting at Anne's is a prototype of what God is really looking for. Although I have not been to Anne's in about eight weeks, I was struck yesterday by the sense of 'family' that was forming. There were some ladies there whose countenance has completely changed, to the point where I hardly recognized them. Women who had initially been so timid and unsure of themselves were confidently giving expression to their thoughts as they were led by the Spirit to do so. The healing that has been going on is at a deep level, and those who have been wounded by institutional church are finding rest and a place to call home."

Needless to say, this email blessed me. It reminded me, though week after week I might not see exactly what God was up to, He *was* up to something. He was healing, transforming, and changing lives—not just mine, but everyone's who came to be part of this time we set apart to be with the Lord, even those who came to visit a time or two. It is marvelous to be about His business and to see and hear of the fruit. We were still right on track and the plan was to keep moving ahead.

A New Year—2006

As the new year began, I was beginning to feel tired. Up to this point, it truly had been effortless setting every Tuesday aside for meetings, getting my house ready, coordinating the schedules, transcribing teachings, and planning for lunch. Anywhere from fifteen to thirty women were coming on Tuesday mornings. When you are operating with the leading of the Holy Spirit, there is an effortlessness about all you have to do. But when the ease to which you have operated lessens and your tasks become more like a responsibility, it might be a sign it is time to shake things up a bit and move into a new direction. In that I was beginning to grow a bit weary, I decided I needed to let the group know how I was feeling. I was also dealing with a physical issue that needed to be addressed, and it looked like I was going to have some surgery.

I asked the women to begin praying about shifting our meetings from once a week to once every two weeks. It was an idea that "dropped into my thinking," to quote Carol Grier, and I felt peace about it. However, that request caused anxiety for some. We all had grown very dependent on our meetings each week. For two years, we had operated with a regular routine of meeting on Tuesday mornings and there was an expectation, I think, that this would continue. We were used to being together every week. Although I was a bit nervous about suggesting we shift our meetings to twice a month, I knew the Lord would correct us if we made a wrong move.

It did not take long for everyone to be on board, which served as some good confirmation to me that this was all OK. The meetings changed to every other week, and we soon got into a new rhythm. "They devoted themselves to the apostles' teaching and to the fellowship, to the breaking of bread and to prayer. Everyone was filled with awe, and many wonders and miraculous signs were done by the apostles. All the believers were together and had everything in common. Selling their possessions and goods, they gave to anyone as he had need. Every day they continued to meet together in the temple courts. They broke bread in their homes and ate together with glad and sincere hearts, praising God and enjoying the favor of all the people. And the Lord added to their number daily those who were being saved." (Acts 2:42-47)

In April, I had minor surgery. Sharon Lampke, one of the Glory Girls, offered to open her home to host the meetings, so the meetings continued. My surgery was successful and I found that the rest and recovery was a needed respite. My recovery took a little longer than expected, but by the end of May I was up and running again, and free to begin hosting the meetings again.

As the year continued, we hosted several other speakers, but we also opened the floor to women in our own group who had teachings to share with us, and several times this occurred. Connie May put together a teaching for us based on Psalm 127. Psalm 127 has always been one of my favorite Scriptures. Below is what she shared with us one Tuesday morning.

Connie May–Teaching from Psalm 127

"Unless the Lord builds the house, its builders labor in vain.
Unless the Lord watches over the city, the watchmen stand
guard in vain.
In vain you rise early and stay up late, toiling for food to eat—
for he grants sleep to those he loves.
Sons are a heritage from the Lord, children a reward from him.
Like arrows in the hands of a warrior are sons born in one's
youth.
Blessed is the man whose quiver is full of them.
They will not be put to shame when they contend with their
enemies in the gate." (Ps. 127)

Jesus' teaching on the two foundations is found in Matthew
7:24-27. Jesus said, "Therefore everyone who hears these words
of mine and puts them into practice is like a wise man who built
his house on the rock. The rain came down, the streams rose,
and the winds blew and beat against that *house*; yet it did not
fall, because it had its foundation on the rock. But everyone who
hears these words of mine and does not put them into practice
is like a foolish man who built his house on sand. The rain came
down, the streams rose, and the winds blew and beat against
that house, and it fell with a great crash."

This house of faith is our belief system. It is where the real
you lives! Think of it as a dwelling place. It is a safe place. It is
where you house or keep your private thoughts, dreams, fears,
hopes, and joys. The Bible calls this *the true you* or *the hidden
man of the heart.* Our ideas and thoughts about life begin forming even before you are born. If our experiences in life are good,
then we feel safe to share our thoughts, dreams, fears, hopes,
and joy with others. Pretty soon, we learn who is safe to share
those things with and who is not. This forms our belief system.
One of the problems with living in a fallen world is it is forever
changing, and so are the people around us, so it can be confusing to know what to believe.

Once we become Christians, we have already built or established
a lot of views about life. Our belief system is formed and works
to keep us safe. So when we begin to read the Bible, it may be

that we are not sure what to believe. What is true? What is trustworthy? In Romans 12, we see this is called the "renewing of our mind." When we base our belief upon the truth found in God's Word, then our faith in Him will stand during the storms of life, and we too will come through the storms intact. We may not have liked the storm, but our trust in God is keeping us safe.

Life and death are part of life. We are not guaranteed our children will live to be eighty-seven, or that our spouses will always be there for us. Much of life is uncertain. It is our belief system that connects us to God. He created us, or designed us, to be close to Him through all of life. He desires to keep us safe and steady during the storms of life. He is our loving Father, but the choice is ours. Do we want to invest in that relationship?

We all know it is not easy to build a house, or even get a tent set up in a storm. Everything gets real messed up. Rain and mud get everywhere. Some things even get ruined. That is also true when we wait and try to figure out what we believe is true about God when things in our life are like a storm. Then we wonder, "What are His promises? Where is He?" In the storm, life as we know it changes rapidly. Everything seems wrong, and it is hard to find the next step. This is not the best time to try and build.

It is best to seek these answers and establish your foundation in the quiet moments. Jesus says, "Ask and it will be given you; seek and you will find; knock and the door will be opened to you. For everyone who asks receives; he who seeks finds; and to him who knocks, the door will be opened." (Matt 7:7-8) I think it is interesting that Jesus said this just a few verses before He taught about the two foundations in Matthew 7:24-27!

Notice that the wise man's foundation is built on *the words of Jesus*. His words are true. They are spirit and they are life. (John 6:63) He is the way, the truth, and the life. He is the only way to the Father. (John 14:6)

His truth is unchanging. It is the only stable foundation to build upon. It is built one truth at a time. The first truth is God is love! (1 John 4:8) All other truths are built on this one. It is essential we have this settled forever, otherwise, when the storm hits, we will not want to draw near Him.

We have been talking about life in His kingdom and the laws that govern His kingdom. We want His kingdom to come, and His will to be done, on earth as it is in heaven (Matthew 6:10). **Our faith is the key that connects us to His kingdom.** We can use the key, or we can set it aside and wait for another day. The choice is ours. Choose to be a wise woman (man). Choose to build your house of faith. It will be a safe place for you and Your God to dwell.

Faith is built by spending time in His Word. His Word (the Rock) plus the mortar (time spent with Him) equals you being safe and secure in the Father's Love. (Ps. 91)

This season in the life of the Glory Girls was just as special as all the others had been. It was exciting to see the women in our group begin to step out and share their gifts and talents. It was a continual part of the on-going training the Lord has us in. And His blessing on this time we set apart for Him was evident and sure.

Reflection

What do you believe? What does the foundation you stand upon look like? Is it a foundation built on self? Pride? Monetary value? Beauty? Intellect? Is your foundation built on your position? The value and worth you put in your status? I want to suggest to you today, that if these are things you are standing on, they will not save you when the rain and the storms come. As I am writing, an earthquake has just occurred in Japan. A tsunami resulted, causing catastrophic devastation. No money, no status, no beauty, no intellect—none of these things can help you when things like this happen. Today, reflect on Psalm 46 and Psalm 121. My hope and prayer for you is that you can come into a real understanding of Whom you should build your foundation upon—Jesus Christ. He is solid. He is true. He is real. He is the Son of the living God. "Turn your eyes upon Jesus, look full in His wonderful face, and the things of the earth will grow strangely dim in the light of his glory and grace."[11]

Prayer

Heavenly Father, I come before You today realizing I have put a lot of value in a foundation that is not trustworthy, solid, or safe. Forgive me Lord. I want to ask for Your help. Help me let go of those things that I value which are really a false security. I am asking You to help me begin to put in place a solid foundation on which to stand. You are the Rock. And Your Word offers a solid, safe foundation on which to build. I know that You will sustain me while I am here on earth and provide for me a glorious life eternal with You. I need You to lead, guide, and direct me Holy Spirit, as I begin to remove those things that rust and moths can destroy. (Matt. 6:19) Help me this day begin building a strong spiritual home on a solid foundation. I ask this in Jesus' Name. Amen

Suggested Bible Reading

Matthew 6:19-24; 1Timothy 6:3-21; Psalm 91

CHAPTER 14

Listening Prayer

IN EARLY 2007, AS WE gathered together to pray and ask the Lord for His direction for us, Carol Grier felt led to share a new concept with us. Carol is a Christian counselor, and she and her co-workers had started gathering once a week to listen to what the Lord had to say. They would then write down what they heard and go around the room sharing with one another what the Lord had said. She told us how powerful those gatherings had become as they pur-posed to sit still and listen to the Holy Spirit. Carol wondered if this was something we should try, and we all agreed we should. Thus began a new three-year season of what we called Listening Prayer.

This new season was awesome! The Lord would give us each a word, or a picture, a Scripture, or a song, something we would be able to share with one another. As we would begin to share these visions and words, we could see a common theme unfold before us. I had an immediate desire to compile all the words so we could re-read them when we wanted to. So each time we met, the women would email the words they had gotten that day, and I would put them together in the order they had been shared. We began calling these compilations "Listening Prayer Chronicles." There were times the words were a warning. Other times we would hear a message that called us into intercession for a loved one. Other times, He would just pour out His love on us.

The Lord used this Listening Prayer time to fine-tune our ears to hear His voice. There were twelve regulars who were involved in this season of our meetings. From this point on, until our break in 2010, we would begin every meeting this way, unless we hosted a guest or the Holy Spirit had something else in mind for us. It reminds me of a Scripture in Habakkuk 2:1-3: "I will stand at my watch and station myself on the ramparts; I will look to see what he will say to me, and what answer I am to give to this complaint. Then the Lord replied: 'Write down the revelation and make it plain on tablets so that a herald may run with it. For the revelation awaits an appointed time; it speaks of the end and will not prove false. Though it linger, wait for it; it will certainly come and will not delay.'"

As I've said, listening and journaling are important aspects of the Christian life to help deepen your relationship with the Lord. I thought I would take this opportunity to share one of our chronicles with you. This particular morning, we received what we felt was a love letter from the Lord. I would suggest that you sit in a quiet place, and read this letter out loud as if the Lord wrote it just to you. The Lord desires to speak His love to all of us. I pray you will receive all the Truths of these words today. This is how He really feels about you.

As you read through this chronicle, please note that each asterisk (*) means someone new is sharing. The words in italics are words the Lord is speaking and also includes any Scripture recited. Words not in italics are words the person was speaking to the Lord in their heart. Our listening prayer times were very simple. We usually began by listening to worship music. Then, we would invite the Holy Spirit to come. We would get quiet and listen. Each of us would journal what we heard or saw in the Spirit. Once everyone was ready, we would ask the Holy Spirit to lead us in the order we were meant to share. As each one shared, the Lord would begin to paint a picture using similar words or pictures of Scripture as each one shared. It was always a magnificent time. I pray this chronicle will bless you as it did us, and that the Lord will use this word as a word for you today.

Captivate Us Lord Jesus
March 4, 2009

When I captivate you, I draw you in—into My bosom, into My heart, into My arms, into My whole being. It is what I created you for—to be drawn into Me. Imagine My chest with an opening in it, a place you can come into and dwell. I offer rest and peace and love. I offer mercy, forgiveness, and hope. I offer acceptance.

I love you. I created you. I know you. Nothing you do can separate Me from you. You are Mine. I chose you, and invited you to love Me. You accepted My invitation. Oh how I yearn for those who have not. But you, darling one, precious child, you are a daughter of the King. You are My bride. Glory!

So in this quiet moment, as you still your heart and mind let My river of love rush over you. Let Me slip My yoke on your shoulders. It is easy and light. Let My compassion for you burn like a fire—My compassion burning off the dross.

I am always here. My desires for you never change. I love you so deeply—deeper than the ocean. Receive My love, and allow Me to captivate your whole being. I will never leave you nor forsake you. I will only love you, nurture you, hold you, care for you, provide for you, forgive you, bless you, and stand with you. I am yours, now and forever. I am yours, and you will always be Mine.

*Lord, my desire is so strong for You. I feel the warmth of Your presence as You hold me close. I hand You my heart, and You blow the dust off. I am so safe with You. You bring us fresh revelation of who You are, and how much You love us. Saturate us Lord. We are ready. We want more. Release us from the shackles of the world, and tether us to You, Lord Jesus.

I am giving each of you a crown of fragrant flowers as a symbol of My love for you. You are carriers of My fragrance. I am looking for an authentic bride. I will not be counterfeited. I know who's Mine. You are Mine. Rest. Walk. Rest. Walk knowing that you are carriers of My fragrance.

Rest. Ready. Rush. Rest now to get ready for the rush of the new I am sending. Only by resting in Me will you be ready—ready to hear a new thing, ready to see a new way, ready to smell, discern contrary ways, ready to stand in the rush of it all. You are My beloved, although you often don't feel as though you are. In this new rush, you will begin to see how valuable and precious you are to Me. Beloved, you BE loved, you BE strong, you BE secured, you BE relieved of fear and doubt, you BE wrapped in glory and grace, you BE Mine. You belong to Me.

I'm your Knight in shining armor. When you were alone, lost, afraid, and hungry in the forest, I found you, and I rescued you. I will protect you, comfort you, hold you, lead you, sing to you, defend you, make you smile and sing again. I will die for you.

Lord God, what do I love more, Your strength or Your gentleness, Your justice or Your mercy, Your discipline or Your tenderness, Your judgment or Your grace? In Your loving care, I lack for nothing. If I choose, I am never hungry or thirsty. We're only ever parted from you because we turn from You. You never ever leave us.

Be strong and courageous. Do not be terrified. Do not be discouraged. The Lord your God will be with you wherever you go.

Captivate us, Lord Jesus, with You. Devastate us, with Your presence. Holy fountain, consume us with You, with You. Anointed hands; fragrance of the Lord.

Prepare to pray. Peace. Peace, be still. Gently quiet. Full of light.

Radiance. "*Finally, be strong in the Lord and in his mighty power. Put on the full armor of God so that you can take your stand against the devil's schemes. For our struggle is not against flesh and blood, but against the rulers, against the authorities, against the powers of this dark world and against the spiritual forces of evil in the heavenly realms. Therefore put on the full armor of God, so that when the day of evil comes, you may be able to stand your ground, and after you have done everything, to stand. Stand firm then, with the belt of truth buckled around your waist, with the breastplate of righteousness in place, and with your feet fitted with the readiness that comes from the gospel of peace. In addition to all this, take up the shield of faith, with which you can extinguish all the flaming arrows of the evil one. Take the helmet of salvation and the sword of the Spirit, which is the word of God. And pray in the Spirit on all occasions with all kinds of prayers and requests. With this in mind, be alert and always keep on praying for all the saints.*" (Eph. 6:10-18)

*We seek You Lord, desiring only to be in Your presence and to seek Your face, to behold Your beauty, Your glory, to be enslaved by Your love. We seek to die to any false identity and to be so enmeshed with You, that our true identity comes forth from being connected with You. Only in that relationship can we live from our truest selves, our pure soul which was with You from the foundation of the world, the soul that must remain intimately connected with You in order to find itself and to restore its original purity. We will come to You as little children, to dance and sing and twirl, to live with You in the great adventure, to seek the role You created us for. To believe that, finding that will change the world in some way, the way You intended. We desire to learn to trust our hearts, to live from our hearts for that is where You dwell. To learn to recognize the language You speak to us, and the ways You come to us. We know You are the One who loves us most and best. We desire to minister to Your heart. You are our hero! We lift our face to You. We can't live if we move out of Your arms.

Child, O child, you are more to Me than the stars in the heavens.

O how I love you, My children, My body, My church, My Bride. The wedding is coming. It is imminent. The procession has begun. That is why I've started sending gifts—manifestations of My glory. In the coming months you will begin to see reports of them from all around your nation—a new thing. Many will reject these gifts because of their legalistic and intellectual mindsets. Pray that most will receive and benefit, being changed, sanctified, healed by My gifts. They are for Bridal preparation. Many have been invited by Satan to open the door to depression and hopelessness. I say to you, the joy of the Lord is your strength. Your joy and faith in these turbulent times is a light shining in the darkness, though some may deem that hope foolish. Wisdom and truth are proven by their fruit. You are a tree planted by the river, which bears fruit in season and out.

I see a picture of people as holy trees with arms lifted worshipping, offering fruit to God.

This is life as I intended—Me shining life, giving sun, and raining to nourish. I am also the soil beneath you, which gives you foundation and nutrients. If you receive, then you will bear. In worship, in offering the fruit back, you begin the cycle anew.[12]

Reflection

Now is time for you to take a shot at Listening Prayer. You may have already started to journal your thoughts, but today is time to ask the Lord for a specific word. If you are meeting with a group, suggest the Listening Prayer discipline to the group. Whether you sit still as an individual or together as a group, all you have to do is invite the Holy Spirit to come, and then be still and listen. Journal what you hear and then go around the room allowing each one to share in the order they feel the Lord is leading. I promise you, it will be a total blessing.

God does speak, and you can hear His voice. I do want to remind you that no two people will hear the same way. Some may journal single words. Others may only see in pictures, so they will journal what they saw. Still others may write a piece of prose. And some may hear a hymn or a song. Please note, just because the song is not a worship song or a hymn does not mean it is not from God. God can use everyday music to get His point across. If the Spirit keeps repeating a Scripture to you, write it down. All are good to share, and all are from the Spirit. So give it a go. And invite the Lord to give you a personal word today whether you are by yourself or in a group setting. Relax and let the Holy Spirit flow.

Prayer

Holy Spirit, come. Release Your revelatory word over me today I pray in Jesus' Name. Thank You that I do have ears to hear You speak. Thank You that I can hear Your voice. In the name of Jesus, I come against any thoughts or belief systems that say I cannot hear You. That is a lie. Speak to me Lord. Your words are living water. Quench my thirst today Jesus, as I sit at Your feet and hear what You have to say. Captivate me, Lord Jesus. Draw me in closer to You. I ask this in Your precious Name. Amen.

Suggested Bible Reading

Song of Solomon

Other Books

The Voice of God by Cindy Jacobs

CHAPTER 15

A Step Out In Faith

GODFREY BIRTILL'S WORSHIP MUSIC HAD become an integral part of the life of the Glory Girls. When John Scotland first introduced Godfrey's music to us, we were immediately attracted to its raw sound and life-giving lyrics. The Lord seemed to continually use lyrics from Godfrey's songs to speak to us. So one day, sisters Ann Henderson and Carol Grier decided to email Godfrey on a whim to let him know how much his music was impacting our prayer group and them personally. Would you believe, Godfrey replied back to them. We were so excited when they told us they had heard back from him, we encouraged Ann and Carol to write him again to ask if he would ever be interested in coming to Charlotte to visit our prayer group. Sure enough, he not only responded, but said he would be willing to come meet us. He had plans to be in the states at the end of February 2008, and said he could pass through Charlotte to spend a day and night with us. We were thrilled! With this fantastic opportunity on the horizon, we began to pray for God's will for this visit, asking the Lord to go before us and prepare the way.

Ann and Carol worked in high gear preparing for Godfrey's visit, and I asked them if they would like some help organizing the logistics of his visit. They said, "Yes," so for the next several months, Ann, Carol, and I would meet and pray and talk in hopes of discerning what this visit should look like. And when our prayer group met, we would intercede for this visit as well.

In times like these you have an opportunity to encounter God's trustworthiness and faithfulness, and we did at a deep level. We knew the daytime meeting was covered. We planned to host Godfrey in my home with the morning prayer group. However, as we began looking for a venue for an evening meeting, we could not find any churches willing to host the worship event. I imagine it seemed a bit odd to invite someone to come to town we had never met, and then try and find a church to host him for a worship service. We only knew Godfrey through John Scotland and through his music. This is a picture of what stepping out in faith can look like. We were moving in the direction the Holy Spirit was leading us, not relying on our own intellect and understanding. It may have looked like we were taking a chance, but we really believed we were heading the way the Lord directed so we persevered.

Faith involves believing God can do what you may think is impossible. It makes me think of the story in Matthew 9 when Jesus asked the two blind men who wanted to be healed, "Do you believe that I am able to do this?" When they answered, "Yes, Lord," Jesus heard them and then said, "According to your faith will it be done to you."

Faith also involves action: "You see that his faith and his actions were working together, and his faith was made complete by what he did." (James 2:22) On the outside, our actions may not have looked wise, but sometimes it is those foolish-looking ideas that confound the wise and bring real blessings and life. "Brothers, think of what you were when you were called. Not many of you were wise by human standards; not many were influential; not many were of noble birth. But God chose the foolish things of the world to shame the wise; God chose the weak things of the world to shame the strong." (1 Cor. 1:26-27)

All the Glory Girls trusted the Lord in this endeavor. We prayed that if this visit was of God, that no weapon would be allowed to form against it. And we prayed that if this visit was not of God, He would clearly show us and shut the door. We believed with all our heart that God was in this. All we needed to do was move ahead.

Now I am not saying it was always easy. There were times we did question ourselves. There were times we voiced our concerns to one another. There were times we wondered if we were really hearing correctly. Each of those times we prayed for the Lord to help keep us on track and show us the way. Sure enough, He did. Proverbs 16:3-4 says: "Commit to the Lord whatever you do, and your plans will succeed. The Lord works out everything for his own ends." Psalm 37:5-6 says: "Commit your way to the Lord; trust in him and he will do this: He will make your righteousness shine like the dawn, the justice of your cause like the noonday sun." We were learning at a deeper level what it looked like to follow the lead of the Holy Spirit. "Trust and obey, for there's no other way to be happy in Jesus, but to trust and obey."[13]

As the day approached for Godfrey's arrival, the only plan we seemed to be able to put in place was a morning meeting at my house. Although Godfrey had voiced an interest in having an evening gathering as well, we simply could not find a place we could afford to rent and we could not find a church willing to open their doors to us. It was time for some Divine intervention.

A week before Godfrey was to visit, Jiljane Brace, who is a dear friend and a Glory Girl who does not live year-round in Charlotte, arrived back in town. We did not know she was in town, so Carol was surprised when she ran into her at the grocery store her first day back.

Carol told Jiljane about Godfrey's visit and our challenge to find a place to host him, his son Michael, and their band mate Steve for an evening worship service. Without any hesitation, Jiljane offered to host them in her beautiful home. It was perfect! Mission accomplished.

We've talked earlier about waiting on the Lord. This time of waiting and trusting proved to solidify what we already knew. "The Lord longs to be gracious to you; he rises to show you compassion. For the Lord is a God of justice. Blessed are all who wait for him!" (Isa. 30:18) On the evening of March 5, Godfrey arrived in Charlotte for his first visit to the Queen City. He was en route from Philadelphia to Atlanta, so Charlotte was a perfect pit stop for him. The next morning, he was in my home, meeting all of us for the first time and leading a group of women in worship. We had a grand morning getting to know him and listening to him sings his songs that we had come to know and love and connect with.

Godfrey Birtill

Godfrey Birtill was born in Chorley, Lancashire, England. He now lives in Lincoln, UK with his wife Gill. He has quite an interesting background. His family has Moravian roots dating back to the early 1700's, and one of his ancestors is Moravian hymn writer James Montgomery, the writer of the hymn, "Angels from the Realms of Glory." "It has been said that Godfrey's unique 'minstrel anointing', blending worship and intercession, is in part an inheritance from his Moravian roots. Much of Godfrey's ministry is connected to 'grass roots' city prayer gatherings across the denominations. He often writes songs on location that are connected to the city, seeking to release the cities indigenous song and lament. He's led worship and done 'Song and Intercession' workshops across the U.K., South Africa, Europe, and America, including song workshops on a reservation with Navajo Indians."[14]

As Godfrey shared a bit about himself, his music, and his ministry with us, he admitted that he was excited to hear that our home group meetings were made up of women from many different denominations and backgrounds. He called us a pioneering group and talked to us about the importance of worship to not only deepen our faith but to also bless the land on which we lived.

Godfrey told us that he used to be a professional photographer. He remembered a time when he encountered an amateur photographer scouting out an event. He said that at this particular point in his own career, photography had become boring, but what he noticed was to this young amateur, photography was exciting. Godfrey said the young man's passion and zeal, his wildness, was so evident that it was irritating. Godfrey then suggested that church should be more amateur than professional. "I want you to pursue amateurism," he said. "So many churches are pursuing professionalism. We need to protect the wild sound, that wild passion for Jesus."

Godfrey opened worship with a hymn his ancestor, James Montgomery wrote. The song is titled "Lift Up Your Heads (Alleluia)," and Godfrey read the lyrics as a prophetic proclamation over the city of Charlotte. "The songs we sing can be tools we use to focus not only on the Lord but to also focus on the land," he said. "We can speak to the land and declare to it that, 'the cross is in the field,'" he said, quoting one of his own songs. "'It is time to turn the battle at the gates.'"[15] Waking up the land with songs we sing or words we pray was a new thought for me. I imagine it was for many others as well. Godfrey was sharing new revelation and we were all ears.

As the song lyrics were handed out for us to sing, Godfrey invited us to press in to the presence of God and worship together. "We need to break off fear of man that is a snare and makes us afraid of our own voices. It is time to be free, recognizing that when we sing and when we pray, we can see the foundations change in the city. We can see doors open. We can see an awakening to the land. It is time for the church to rise up and speak out," Godfrey said. "It is time to speak prophetically over the land. If you don't, someone else will." Thus began a wonderful morning of singing praises to the Lord and prophetic words over the city of Charlotte.

"Lift Up Your Heads (Alleluia)"

Lift up your heads, you gates of brass!
You bars of iron yield!
And let the King of glory pass;
The cross is in the field.

Alleluia…Alleluia…Alleluia….Alleluia
Alleluia…Alleluia….Alleluia…..Alleluia

You armies of the living God
Stand in your Captains might
Go where no hallowed feet had trod
Arise My warrior Bride!

O fear not, faint not, halt not now;
Don't quit, like men be strong,
To Christ shall every nations bow,
And sing with you this song.

Uplifted are the gates of brass
The bars of iron yield.
Behold the King of Glory pass.
The cross is in the field.[16]

© 2003 Thankyou Music UK

As we continued singing his songs, we realized Godfrey was weaving together a message that centered on waking up the land and the people to respond to God. It was a wonderful time. We ended the meeting with lunch and a good time of fellowship. It was great getting to meet the man behind the music we had grown to appreciate, and we were excited about our evening event. Godfrey, Michael, and Steve eventually headed back to their hotel to rest, and we prepared for the evening meeting at Jiljane's home.

Evening Meeting

That night at Jiljane's, Godfrey's energy and enthusiasm was contagious. We had a large crowd and had a great time singing and worshipping together. Godfrey shared a bit more about himself and talked about what he had been seeing in the church as he traveled around the globe. After a while, Godfrey began to preach from Mark 5:1-20. In this story, Jesus comes into a town and finds a demon-possessed man who had been living in the tombs. Godfrey suggested that this story tells us about the sound of the land. "Land has a sound. Land has a voice," he said. "A city has its own sound; Charlotte has its own voice, its own vibe. We read in Hosea 4:3, 'Therefore the land mourns, and everyone who lives in it languishes along with the beasts of the field and the birds of the sky, and also the fish of the sea disappear.'" (Hos. 4:3 NASB) Again, this new revelation about land was being presented. It was a fascinating thought, and we listened as Godfrey went on to explain what he meant.

"So here is this place we read about in Mark, the Gerasenes, and Jesus all of a sudden comes along. We see that when Jesus comes to town, things begin to change. In this passage, we see that the demonic stronghold 'Legions' does not want Jesus to come to town. Why? Because they know that when Jesus comes to town, His presence comes too, and that means their time is up. When Jesus comes to town, people are going to be set free." Godfrey said that it's not just people and cities that don't want Jesus to come to town; some churches don't want him either. They prefer to stay the way they are too. They don't want change because they don't want things messed up from the way they have been operating. It makes me think of the new wine skin and the old wine skin that we talked about earlier and we read about in Luke 5:36-38.

In this story from Mark, not only do the demons plead for Jesus to leave, but also the people of the city plead with Jesus to leave after He has healed the demoniac. That's an interesting response, isn't it? I had never looked at this passage in this light. "I believe there is something connected to the fact that the people of the area give the authority," Godfrey continued. "It shows us that the people in the area have a massive sway on what stays in a city and what goes out of a city. The people of the area have the authority for the demonic to stay or to go. The people of that area were quite happy with the man being off his head and out of his mind and with that Legion being in that area. You see, when Jesus sent the demonic stronghold named "Legions" out of the man and into the pigs, and those pigs went off the cliff, well, that was a lot of money and security that went off the cliff. Gone. So this is what the sound of the land looked like," Godfrey said. "They did not want Jesus to be there. They did not want His presence. They did not like what they saw happening and they wanted Him to leave. They did not like what was happening… their finances going over the cliff. Things were getting messed up."

"When revival breaks out," he continued, "some people are not going to like it. Some people will say, 'Stop it.' But others will dance and announce, 'A wildfire is coming!' I am believing for a wildfire. So if you want Jesus here in Charlotte, if that is how you are praying, get ready, because when Jesus comes to town, things change. Maybe for revival to break out in Charlotte, the finances are going to be affected. This Scripture is a prophetic Scripture—and when we call on the presence of God, it does not mean things will always get better. There may be some shaking that occurs. When Jesus comes to town, there is a release of the supernatural. People are set free from the things that hold them in bondage. It's like a revolution. When we pray, 'Your kingdom come, Your will be done,' now *that's* a revolution."

The night continued with Godfrey leading us in intercession for the city of Charlotte, singing many of the songs he has written, ending the evening singing his song, "I Stand." There was intensity and electricity as we proclaimed Jesus over the land and over the city of Charlotte. To be together, unified in intercession is a powerful thing, and all of us were blessed as a result. "Again, I tell you that if two of you on earth agree about anything you ask for, it will be done for you by my Father in heaven. For where two or three come together in my name, there I am with them." (Matt 18:19-20)

All in all, it was a fantastic first meeting. Godfrey encouraged us, blessed us, and taught us about the power of praying for our city and the land. He headed on to Atlanta the next day, but we kept in touch and hosted him again a year later. As his ministry and his music have become more known in our area, several other churches have hosted him since our first meeting. We count Godfrey as a friend and still enjoy his music.

Reflection

Do you like to sing? Then you may be a worshipper at heart. Scripture tells us that God inhabits the praises of His people. He loves for us to worship Him in song. Think about David. With harp in hand, he blessed the Lord with his singing. Whether it is singing hymns from your church hymnbook, or praising God singing a contemporary Christian song, you need to know that the Lord loves it when we worship Him this way. So branch out of your box and browse some Christian artists on iTunes or in the bookstore. You can find anything from hard Christian rock to quiet, contemplative Christian music. I have listed some of my personal favorites in the back in the Resource section. And start to sing! "Sing to the Lord, you saints of his; praise his holy name." (Ps. 30:4)

Prayer

Thank you Lord that music is known as the universal language. I pray today that the heart of worship would be released in my life, in Jesus' Name. Use the lyrics and the music of songs to speak to me Lord. Give me the ears to hear Your message in them. Thank You Lord for the sound of music. May I open myself up even more to You through worship in song. I ask this in Jesus' Name. Amen

Suggested Bible Reading

Psalm 66:1-4; Psalm 98

"I Will Stand"

After I've done everything, I will stand
With my eyes on the King of Kings, I will stand.... I will stand.
I will stand in confidence
To see the Lord's deliverance
I will stand.... I will stand.
Of this I am absolutely sure
I'll see the goodness of the Lord
Yes I will stand.

Because I'm standing with Jesus
I am standing with my King
Because I'm standing with Jesus
I am standing with my King.

Even in the darkest days, I will stand
And bring a sacrifice of praise, I will stand.... I will stand.
No matter what is thrown at me
I'll stand against the devil's schemes
I will stand.... I will stand.
Upright and undisturbed
Unafraid I'm standing firm
Yes I will stand. [17]

Godfrey Birtill
© 2003 Thankyou Music UK

CHAPTER 16

The Calm in the Storm

THE YEAR 2008 WAS INTERESTING for me personally. I turned fifty (which was wonderful) and I was also diagnosed with melanoma (which was not so wonderful). I want to take some time to share what happened so you can see that God is always present.

I grew up in Roanoke, Virginia. I still keep in touch with many of the people I grew up with and went to school with. In 2005, a group of old girlfriends decided that we needed to take a weekend away at the beach to hang out and spend time together. Thus began our annual beach trip to Wrightsville Beach in North Carolina.

This particular year, we were enjoying our regular routine of shopping, shopping, shopping, and meal planning. On Saturday evening, while we were on the porch having a cocktail at the end of the day, one of my friends, Sallie Lake, happened to notice a mole on top of my left ear. "AG," (AG is my nickname from high school days) "you better get that mole on your ear checked out. It doesn't look good," she said. Everyone looked at it and I, of course, had no idea it was even there because it was on the top of my ear and I could not see it. I told her I would get it checked out. As a matter of fact, I had scheduled six months earlier an appointment to go see my dermatologist, and it happened to fall the day after I got home from this beach trip.

So that Monday, I went in to see my dermatologist, Patty Roddey. I told her about what Sallie had said, and asked her to look at the mole on my ear. Initially, she didn't think anything of it, but after checking me all over, she came back to it and said, "Let's go on and biopsy it just in case." You can imagine my shock when the phone rang two days later with the news that the lab results had come back, and the mole was cancerous. It was melanoma.

What happened next was surreal as events began to quickly unfold. Patty gave me the name and number of a plastic surgeon, and scheduled me to meet with him on Friday. She said this kind of cancer was nothing to mess around with and I needed to be seen ASAP. When I hung up, I felt sort of numb, but also unaware of what all this really could mean. I got right back into my usual routine, but decided to email a few of the Glory Girls to let them know what was up and to ask them to begin praying for me. I continued to stay busy until the music teacher showed up for the kids' guitar lessons that afternoon. When they were settled in to the lesson, I went into my bedroom and got still. I shut my eyes to begin letting the news sink in. Next thing I knew, I was having a vision.

I saw a huge boulder, and then a very large male lion with a full mane jumped up on the boulder and sat down. He began to roar. I just watched as he let out this thundering roar over and over again. Then the lion jumped off of the boulder and strode off into the darkness. The scene then turned very dark and all I could see was the outline of the lion wrestling with something.

Carol Grier called soon thereafter. She had seen my email, and was calling to check in with me. I shared the vision with her that I had just had. Immediately she began reciting Psalm 23:5: "You prepare a table before me in the presence of my enemies." We talked about the lion representing the Lion of Judah, the Lord. A lion also represents courage and boldness. The boulder made me think of Jesus. We read in 1 Corinthians 10:4: "They drank from the Spiritual rock that accompanied them, and that rock was Christ."

I felt this vision was a sign from the Lord that He was with me and would be fighting for me. Carol's words from Psalm 23 were an added blessing. I felt complete and supernatural peace. Later on, Glory Girl Niki Hardy also called. She too had a word for me. It was from Revelations 2:7. "He who has an ear, let him hear what the Spirit says to the churches. To him who overcomes, I will give the right to eat from the tree of life, which is in the paradise of God." This word also gave me such peace, and I began decreeing that I was and am an over-comer.

The next day as I was sitting alone in my kitchen, the Holy Spirit began to speak to me. This is what He said: "Anne, you are My child of light in the darkness. Do not be afraid. You can hear Me. You will hear Me. I AM your Rock. I AM roaring. I AM roaring and I AM warring in the heavenlies for you. I AM victorious." I sat in the quiet and let those words penetrate in my body and soul. I've got to tell you, there is nothing like getting a word from the Lord. That is why it is so important to be able to hear His voice. He is the calm in the storm. He is the light in the darkness.

Friday was another busy day and I still don't think the news had really sunk in. At this point, I had not had a good cry. But after meeting with the surgeon, the floodgates opened. That poor doctor. I was completely taken aback when I heard how much of my ear he was going to have to remove, and I have to be honest, vain thoughts began rushing through my mind. "What will I do about my hair? Will I have to start coloring it again? No more earrings? What will it look like? What will *I* look like?" The thoughts went on and on. I got home and realized I was in a state of panic. And then the phone rang.

It was Carol again and she had another word for me. She read Psalm 110:1-2 to me over the phone which says: "The Lord says to my Lord: 'Sit at my right hand until I make your enemies a footstool for your feet. The Lord will extend your mighty scepter from Zion; you will rule in the midst of your enemies.'" And even now, writing this out, I am reminded of the Scripture verse that was prophesied over me in September 2002 at the Chavda conference from Deuteronomy 33:27: "The eternal God is your refuge, and underneath are the everlasting arms. He will drive out your enemy before you, saying, 'Destroy him!'" Wow. What an amazing blessing. Once again, peace came rushing in.

I decided it was time to let some more people know what was happening. I am not one to keep things like this to myself. I *know* about the power of prayer. I sat down and wrote an email to all the Glory Girls, the Butterflies, the Roanoke girls, and several other girlfriends telling them what was going on and asking them to pray for me. The weekend was approaching. It was my daughter Hallie's thirteenth birthday and it was also Mother's Day weekend. The prayer request was sent and the peace had returned, so I simply got into the moment and decided to embrace all that was happening for the weekend. God was in charge and I was not going to spend the weekend in anxiety or worry.

On Saturday morning, I ended up having some more unexpected quiet time with the Lord. As I began to talk to the Father, I found myself saying these words: "I would not be telling You the truth if I said I didn't hope and wish that You would heal me and supernaturally take this cancer away. But I want You to know, it's OK if You don't." And then I got still having realized what I just said: "It's OK if You don't." Suddenly, in that moment, I realized I had really gotten to a place where I knew who God was and how much He loved me. I don't know if that makes sense to you, but for me, there was total trust. I knew enough about His character to have complete confidence that He would take care of me. I did not know if this cancer was from sun damage from years of living in Virginia Beach and frying my skin, or if it was hereditary, or maybe it was just one of those things that happen that we can't understand this side of heaven. Once again, perfect peace enveloped me.

Later that day, I kept hearing the word "Joshua" in my spirit. I finally went to the book of Joshua to investigate. In Joshua 1:9, it says this: "Be strong and courageous. Do not be terrified; do not be discouraged, for the Lord your God will be with you wherever you go." How about that for a promise?

At church on Sunday, the word had gotten out to a few other folks and I received some good hugs and lots of, "I'm praying for you" words. The Body of Christ can be such a blessing. That night I went to bed and I had a beautiful dream. I was skiing on a luscious green mountain that was dusted with snow. My arms were straight out on either side and as I was skiing down the mountain, I was yelling, 'I'M FREEEEEEEEE." Thank You Jesus!

On Monday, I woke up feeling kind of low, but my email was full of well wishes and positive words. Then I saw a rare and beautiful sight outside: two female and one male rose-breasted grosbeak birds were sitting on one of our bird feeders. It was a sign to me that God was ever-present. Three is the number for the Trinity. The Lord knows how much I love birds. I can watch birds on my bird feeder and get carried into a place of calm and peace. When I happen to see a bird that is rare for our feeder, I truly believe the Lord shows them to me to remind me I can see Him and hear Him. This was a special sighting and one that truly blessed my day.

At lunch, I was just sitting at my kitchen counter when the Spirit began to speak to me again. "Anne, I've set you apart for My own from the beginning, and I will continue to do it My way, in My timing and with My power. You won't miss it. You won't miss out, because I AM in charge of the time and the place and the circumstances. I AM the Alpha. I AM the Omega. With Me, there is beginning and there is end. All things are possible with Me. My ways are right. My kingdom purposes are true, set into motion before the world began. Be strong. Be of good cheer. You are in the palm of My hand."

And sure enough, a little while later, Lisa Hood, another Glory

Girl, wrote me an email and said, "Anne, the Lord is telling me that you are in the palm of His Hand." Don't you just love it? What was curious to me then was of all the things that cancer could have hit, it was my ear that was getting ready to be cut. And yet, my hearing was clearer than ever. "You intended to harm me, but God intended it for good to accomplish what is now being done, the saving of many lives. So then, don't be afraid. I will provide for you and your children." (Gen. 50:20-21) What the enemy might have meant for harm, God was going to use for good.

On Tuesday, I got a call from another dear sister in Christ. She ended up putting such fear in me about my upcoming surgery, I became overcome with worry. It is interesting. I know she meant well, but the outcome was anything but peace. We have to be so careful at times when we speak to others in hopes to comfort.

No sooner did I hang up from her but Connie May, another Glory Girl, called. Perfect timing. Connie used to be a nurse, and as I shared what had just been said to me, she went into intercession on my behalf. She cut me free from all the words that had been spoken to me that caused such unrest and fear. They were not of the Lord. I don't remember her prayer now but I do remember that peace was once again ushered back into my heart. I can honestly say from that moment on, the rest of the week was completely filled with peace.

On Wednesday, the Glory Girls came to my home for a meeting and it was awesome. A great diversion, it was wonderful to be back in the flow of the Spirit with the group. Thursday, my mom came to town to help with the kids and then on Friday at noon, I went in for surgery not knowing what the outcome would be.

Friday morning, when I got up early to get the kids off to school, I saw the phone light blinking on our answering machine. I figured it was probably a message from Glory Girl Libby Walker, because she will hit reply and leave messages on my phone from time to time when she is up late at night. Sure enough it was, and I was caught by surprise. On my phone Libby was speaking words of life to me, and then she said she wanted to play some worship music. Next thing I knew, I was hearing Libby playing a worship song on the piano just for me. It is called "Spirit Song." The first line reads: "O let the Son of God enfold You / With his Spirit and His love / Let Him fill your heart and satisfy your soul / O let Him have the things that hold You / And His Spirit like a dove / Will descend upon your life / And make you whole."[18]

I started weeping. I was so touched and overcome with emotion. And then the Spirit of the Lord began to speak: "Anne, do you believe?"

"Yes," I replied.

"Do you believe I AM who they say I AM?"

"Yes," I said again.

"Then do not lean on your own understanding—the picture that has been presented to you. I told you first thing I was roaring for you and warring for you. Do you believe?"

"Yes Lord, I do."

"Then stand firm. The ground is not shaking because of your circumstances. It is shaking because of My divine intervention. Listen to the melody of heaven again [Libby's song] and the words she spoke to you. They are a gift to you today. I love you child. Believe."

I put my pen down after writing the words the Lord had spoken and would you believe right in front of me was a DVD that some folks had sent to me in a care package from Roanoke. You are going to love this. The DVD was the movie *P.S. I Love You*. Once again, I knew it was a sign from the Lord.

The surgery went just as the doctor expected. When he had finished cutting out all the cancer, which meant cutting off the top half of my ear, he said he was going to begin stitching me up. He said he would do his best to reconstruct my ear with the skin from my earlobe, and said he would try and make a new ear lobe for me as well. No sooner did he finish speaking, than the Lord spoke a clear word to me. This is what He said: "I AM the One who is going to sew you up." With that, I felt my whole body relax and fall back deep into the chair. And there I sat with my eyes closed, praising the Lord and thanking Him for all He was doing for me.

When the stitching was done, I asked the doctor how many stitches he had put in. "About fifty," he said. Fifty is the number for liberty, freedom, jubilee. And of course, I knew that because I had just turned fifty! I felt relieved and so thankful when I was told there was no need for any chemo or radiation. All of the cancer had been contained in that little mole, and it was now gone. With that, I headed home with thanksgiving in my heart and gratitude in my soul.

If you saw me today, I bet you would be hard-pressed to figure out which ear is my new ear. God did sew me up that day and the results are nothing short of miraculous. To date, I have had no other signs of melanoma and quite honestly, I do not expect to. It was quite an experience and a real opportunity to see how faithful the Lord is to carry us through difficult times.

Had I not known the Lord through the Holy Spirit, had I not been able to hear Him when He spoke to me, I am not sure I would have been so peace-filled and calm during this time. Had this happened years earlier, I believe I might have handled things quite differently. I continue to be amazed at how near the Lord is to us. I hope you too will come to know Him as your ever-present help in times of trouble. (Ps. 46:1) My prayer is that everyone would get to know Him deeply and understand the great love He has for His children.

Reflection

Are you facing a hard time in your life? Illness? Divorce? Debt? Cancer? Are you feeling scared? Worried? Anxious because you don't know what the outcome will be and you don't know if you can handle it? Well I am here to tell you that God, the Creator of heaven and earth, is waiting for you to invite Him into the pain, the worry, the anxiety, the fear, or the heartache. His deep desire is to be with us when the waters get choppy, even tumultuous. Call on Him today. Submit your issues to Him. And then allow Him to cradle you under His everlasting arms. Rest in Him, and let Him minister to you and talk to you. He *will* see you through this storm. You may not know how, but He does. His ways are higher and deeper and longer and wider than ours ever could be. Cry out to Him. He is waiting.

Prayer

"Be still, and know that I am God." (Ps. 46:10) Lord, Your name tells us who you are. Jehovah-Jireh, You are the God who provides. El Roi, You are the God who sees all things. El Shaddai, You are the All-Sufficient One. Jehovah-Shalom, You are the Lord of Peace. Jehovah-Rapha, You are the God who heals. Jehovha-Shammah, you are the Lord who is always there. Thank You Lord for loving us so. Bless me with Your everlasting presence today, so that I will know that You are with me in these difficult times. Lord, I ask that You send someone or something across my path this day to comfort me, encourage me, and give me strength. I pray Lord I will see Your goodness and Your provision. You are the best Dad I could ever have. Thank You for being with me Lord, in Jesus' Name. Amen.

"For the Lord comforts his people and will have compassion on his afflicted ones." (Isa. 49:13)

Suggested Bible Reading

Psalm 17:6-8; Psalm 91

CHAPTER 17

Walking in Our Authority

SUMMER CAME AND WENT AND our group kept in touch, meeting for an occasional lunch to catch up and visit. We made our plans for the fall and got right back into meeting once school began again. Opportunities arose to host more visitors, so we continued to open the door for those who were free to come spend a morning with us.

Barry and Mary Kissell–The Shaking

In November, the Glory Girls had the pleasure of hosting Barry and Mary Kissell from St. Mary's Church in London. Barry is the

Associate Rector at St. Mary's, and his wife Mary is in charge of their prayer ministry. Both are gifted and both operate in the prophetic. I had met Barry and Mary several years earlier and had a powerful experience with God through Barry's ministry. So I was thrilled to have the opportunity to host them and have them in my home.

I first met Barry in April 2004. It was what I like to call a Divine encounter. I had accompanied Rob on one of his business trips and had taken a book with me that Barry had written titled, *The Prophet's Notebook*. On the plane coming home from California, I picked up the book and was reading it when I began having a vision. In the vision, I saw a large field full of yellow flowers. It was breathtakingly beautiful. I believed this vision meant I would be receiving a gift as I had come to understand that both flowers and the color yellow usually symbolize a gift from the Lord. I then heard the Holy Spirit speak to me: "Barry will know you. Barry will see you. Barry will have a word for you." This was very interesting to me because I had never met Barry or Mary, but I knew both were in Charlotte, and I was planning to go to hear Barry speak the following night at a gathering.

When I have visions or words from the Lord, I have learned to look at the clock to see the time. The Lord often uses the time on the clock to confirm a word I receive. It was 5:20. Immediately, I thought of 1 Thessalonians 5:20. So I looked it up. 1 Thessalonians 5:20 says: "do not treat prophesies with contempt." The Lord most assuredly had my attention. I began to suspect that I would not only have a chance to meet Barry, but would also have the opportunity for him to pray for me as well. The Lord had a gift for me and Barry was to be the deliverer of the gift. I was expectant and ready to receive it.

The next night, I attended the function where Barry spoke. I arrived at the hotel conference room and took a seat near the front. Barry was pointed out to me by one of the hosts of the event. Within a matter of minutes, Barry approached me. He looked me right in the eye and asked: "Do I know you from somewhere?"

"No," I replied.

"Have we met?" he asked.

"No." I said again.

"Were you at the dinner last night?" he went on.

"No," I answered again, curious about what this could all mean, when suddenly, the words the Holy Spirit spoke to me on the plane the day before came rushing back to my mind: "Barry will know you. Barry will see you. Barry will have a word for you." The words the Spirit had spoken were unfolding one by one. All that was left was for Barry to pray for me, and then I would know what the gift (the field of yellow flowers) was the Lord had in store for me. I told Barry that I was reading his book and we visited a few more minutes until the time came time for Barry to begin his teaching for the evening.

After his talk, Barry invited everyone to stay for prayer and he offered to pray for anyone who wanted ministry. I sat and waited, asking the Lord for His perfect timing. I eventually got up out of my chair and approached Barry. "Do you have any specific prayer needs or requests?" he asked.

"No," I answered, "I just want what the Lord has for me."

With that, Barry laid hands on me and began praying for the Holy Spirit to come. "More power Lord, more power," he said. After just a minute or two, Barry asked, "Do you like to look at birds?"

"Yes," I answered.

"Do you look at them out of your car window?"

"Yes, all the time," I replied grinning and thinking, "how did he know that?"

"Can you call them by name?" he asked.

"Yes, I can," I answered.

At this point, I was beginning to feel the weighty presence of the Lord so heavy on me that I could hardly stand up. Slowly, slowly, I began to bend over. Barry kept asking the Holy Spirit for more power and eventually, I ended up on my knees on the floor.

Then Barry spoke: "You have a strong prophetic calling on your life—a strong prophetic anointing." And that was all it took. The presence of the Lord was so heavy on me, I could hardly move.

Barry left me to go speak words of blessing and prophecy over others. The Holy Spirit's presence was all around me. I then began having tingling in both of my hands. It grew more and more intense until it felt like both hands were the size of baseball catcher's mitts. Vertical and horizontal waves of electricity were flowing through both my hands. I don't know how long I was there on my knees experiencing the power of the Lord run through my hands, but I finally motioned Barry over and told him what was happening. "That's the prophetic gifting," he said. "The Lord is doing something here tonight. Just receive it." And that is exactly what I did. I stayed put and enjoyed this wonderful, powerful encounter with God.

The time came to wrap up the evening, and I had to get up and head home. All the way home, I just thanked the Lord for the gift of His presence that night. By faith, I believed and received Barry's words over me. Remember 1 Thessalonians 5:20: "do not treat prophesies with contempt." So when I heard Barry and Mary were coming back to Charlotte in 2008, you can see why I was happy to host them.

Barry opened the Glory Girl meeting by inviting us to get still so we could listen to what the Spirit was saying. Then he had us share, in a sentence or two, what we heard. "The Lord does nothing without revealing His plan to His servants, His prophets," Barry said. How fun for the Lord to confirm our Listening Prayer model.

We had gotten the word out to the masses about Barry and Mary's visit, so we had a large number of women in attendance. To take the time to go around the room and have everyone share what they heard or saw was such a gift. The common thread in all the sharing was this: "In the shaking that is happening all around us, the Lord's plans will prevail. He is faithful, just, and upright, and His light will shine in the darkness."

The "shaking" we were referring to had to do with all that was happening in the world in 2008. The weather, for one, had been more devastating than in previous years. Hurricanes, tornados, and even wildfires in forty-one states had ravaged the United States, killing hundreds and leaving thousands homeless. There were many shootings recorded, at schools and in homes. Gas prices rose to over $4.00 per gallon in 2008. Crude oil prices rose to $100.00 per barrel for the first time ever. Lehman Brothers declared bankruptcy and Bernie Madoff was sentenced to prison for life. A Fundamentalist Latter Day Saints Ranch in West Texas was raided after allegations of abuse. In China, an earthquake registering 7.9 magnitude killed over fifty thousand people and left five million homeless, and a cyclone in Myanmar killed an estimated 22,000 people. And of course, the election results in 2008 were seen by many as a "shaking," as Barack Obama was elected President of the United States.

Barry spent the morning encouraging us in our commitment to meet together, to listen to what the Lord is saying, and then to share it. In 2 Kings 2, we read that Elijah was in charge of a "company" or school of prophets. This is what Barry said:

> You probably know that in the Old Testament different prophets had schools—schools of prophets—like Elijah had a school of prophets. Isaiah had a school too. What I want to illustrate here is that the Word would come to the school or the company when they came together, kind of like what you all do here. So when you come together in the Word to hear the Word, once you've got the Word, you go out with the Word. The Lord has to tell somebody what He is doing. He doesn't just go around doing a thing wishing you knew about it. He usually tells those who are hanging about waiting on Him. And what you will find—I think this is one of the tests to see if you heard correctly or not—is that people you have absolutely no connection with at all will be saying the same thing because they are a prophetic people too, and the Lord reveals His Word to the prophets. So what I see God doing here, this is like a school, a school of prophets. And together you seek the Lord and together you listen to the Lord and together the word goes out from this place.

Barry was putting words to what we had been experiencing. I cannot count the number of times we as a group would hear a word or a phrase or get a picture during our listening prayer sessions, and in a matter of hours or days, get confirmation from someone else or from another ministry who was hearing or seeing the same thing. Needless to say, it is very confirming and affirming.

One of the ministries we aligned with early on was the Elijah List as I mentioned in Chapter 5. Steve Shultz began this prophetic email ministry years ago and most of our Glory Girl group subscribes to it. Tried and true prophetic men and women send the words they hear from the Lord to Steve and he publishes them with the Spirit's leading on the Elijah List site. The opportunity to connect with other prophetic-minded people through this ministry has been a lifeline for all of us. Many times through the Elijah List, words we had received as a prayer group were confirmed. This is what Barry was talking about.

Another ministry that has blessed our prayer group for years is an email devotion written by Ras and Bev Robinson. Ras began publishing prophetic words in January 2001 and his wife Bev joined him in December 2007. Looking back through my journals, I see I have been receiving words of life and hope through this ministry since 2004. The prophetic words are published as "What The Lord is Saying Today."

Barry also talked to us about what our responsibility looks like when we get a word from the Lord. He suggested that when we get a word, maybe for a Pastor or a leader in the church, our only responsibility is to give the person the word. It *is not* our responsibility to make it happen.

He gave an example of someone who has a dream. The Lord might show you that the dream you have had is a very significant dream and maybe the Lord tells you it is for the church. Barry suggests that when this happens, write it down, date it, and appraise it—look at what the dream means. Then pass it on to the Pastor or leader. And that's it. You don't call the person in a month and ask what he or she has done about it. Our business stops when we give the word. It is then up to the person who received it to act upon it.

Now if the Pastor or leader is open, and his / her heart is right with God, then the word—which is living and active and sharper than any double-edged sword—will be received and go on its way. It's got its own power. It's got its own anointing. So all we have to do is say it and then step back. Barry likened this to a hand grenade. "You throw the word out there and then you get out of the way," he said. "If it is a word from God, it will go off." Although God gives the prophet a word to speak, God sets the time for the word to go off. It could be three months, or it could be five years. The timing of it is none of our business. Only saying it—that is our business. Barry mentioned Isaiah. Isaiah spoke a word that took 750 years to happen. (Isa. 53 and 61) Wow!

Barry shifted gears and had us turn to Hebrews 12:25-29. He wanted to talk to us about the shaking we were sensing and seeing. "See to it that you do not refuse him who speaks. If they [the Israelites] did not escape when they refused him who warned them on earth, how much less will we, if we turn away from him who warns us from heaven? At that time his voice shook the earth, but now he has promised, 'Once more I will shake not only the earth but also the heavens.' The words, 'once more' indicate the removing of what can be shaken—that is, created things—so that what cannot be shaken may remain. Therefore, since we are receiving a kingdom that cannot be shaken, let us be thankful, and so worship God acceptably with reverence and awe, 'for our God is a consuming fire.'"

Scripture tells us that, "the kingdom of God *cannot* be shaken" (Heb. 12:28), but the things of man that are not of God *can* be shaken. That is what Barry believed we were seeing in 2008. And the truth is, the "shaking" continues to this day. At this writing, an earthquake and tsunami have hit Japan and tornados have ravaged the American South killing hundreds. These events could most certainly be considered "a shaking."

Barry suggested that God is also shaking things in the church as well. Organized religion, the status quo, the traditions of man, just don't seem to be cutting it any more for a large number of believers who want to have a deeper and more intimate relationship with Jesus. Barry suggested "a shaking" could be the very thing we need to shake us free us from religiosity and from men's ideas and traditions that do not line up with the will of God. "And what will be left," Barry said, "is Jesus! Jesus, His love, His power and His presence."

In Scripture, we see when there is shaking there is also restoration. That may seem contradictory, but it isn't. Haggai and Zechariah were two of God's prophets, and when God talked to Haggai about the shaking, He gave Zechariah eight visions about the restoration of the New Jerusalem. Once the shaking is completed, the rebuilding can begin.

Barry went on to say that as believers, we must keep our eyes open and watch as the Lord is in the process of gathering us for a time of restoration. He suggested that some of the signs to be on the lookout for are the restoration of the gifts of the Spirit, the ministries of the Spirit, and the power of the Spirit. We see in Zechariah 4:6, God says this restoration is "not by might nor by power, but by my Spirit." It may begin small, but Scripture says " Don't despise these small beginnings, for the Lord rejoices to see the work begin." (Zech. 4:10 NLT) Many of God's beginnings start off in what looks like small and insignificant ways. (Makes me think of the mustard seed again, such a small tiny seed when you first look at it, and yet it grows into "the largest tree in the garden.") Barry reminded us of Jesus and His birth. He was a small baby, and yet, He became the greatest person ever to walk on this earth!

"So when the shaking is happening all around us," Barry said, "it is time to put our trust in the Lord. And we should not just sit and wait for the rebuilding to begin. We need to keep moving. We need to be proactive. Do what your hand finds you to do. Just be sure you are doing it by the Spirit," Barry said. (1 Sam. 10:6-7) "Don't try and initiate something or try something just because it's a good idea. You've got to be sure God is in it, and telling you to do it. Everything's got to be by the Spirit. It's got to be by the Spirit."

Our time with Barry and Mary was so blessed. I am once again amazed at how God's word continues to come back again and give new life even after it was initially released. This word is just as relevant for today. And that is the way the prophetic word works. "'For my thoughts are not your thoughts, neither are your ways my ways,' declares the Lord. 'As the heavens are higher than the earth, so are my ways higher than your ways and my thoughts than your thoughts. As the rain and the snow come down from heaven, and do not return to it without watering the earth and making it bud and flourish, so that it yields seed for the sower and bread for the eater, *so is my word that goes out from my mouth: It will not return to me empty, but will accomplish what I desire and achieve the purpose for which I sent it.*'" (Isa. 55:9-11) (Emphasis added.)

December came and so did the time to wrap up our fifth year of meetings. Who would have known God had all this planned for us? We knew how remarkable this time had been and we felt extremely blessed. "But we ought always to thank God for you, brothers [sisters] loved by the Lord, because from the beginning God chose you to be saved through the sanctifying work of the Spirit and through belief in truth. He called you to this through our gospel, that you may share in the glory of our Lord Jesus Christ." (2 Thess. 2:13-14)

Percy and Sara Jo Burns–Deliverance Ministry

We had another fantastic year of meetings in 2009. We also had the opportunity to host several other speakers and spend time together with the Lord when we met alone. Percy and Sara Jo Burns were one such couple we hosted. When I called to invite them to come, they were so excited to hear about our home meetings, they said yes right off the bat and came to spend a morning with us.

Percy was born in Mississippi. He graduated from Belhaven College in Jackson, Mississippi, and from Austin Presbyterian Theological Seminary in Austin Texas. Percy entered the pastorate in 1966 in New Orleans, Louisiana, and has served in three churches: New Orleans for six and a half years, in Shreveport, Louisiana for eleven and a half years, and in Charlotte, North Carolina for the last twenty years. Percy and Sara Jo were introduced to the Holy Spirit and to the ministry of deliverance in July of 1971. Percy has been faithfully bringing people into the fullness of the Holy Spirit and ministering deliverance ever since then—now almost forty years. Percy and Sara Jo are two of the most kind, real, and life-giving people I have met. As mentioned earlier, deliverance ministry is real, vital, and sometimes necessary for one to walk in healing and wholeness.

Percy and Sara Jo love to testify to the Lord's deliverance and healing power, and Percy spent this particular morning with us giving testimony after testimony of God's faithfulness in setting people free from demonic oppression. Percy is a student of Derek Prince, and though Derek is no longer living, his ministry is thriving. The headquarters for his ministry happens to be right here in Charlotte.

Percy walked us through several Scriptures to confirm the relevance of deliverance ministry today. He also said that there seems to be many times a connection between physical healing and deliverance. "He [Jesus] went down with them and stood on a level place. A large crowd of his disciples was there and a great number of people from all over Judea, from Jerusalem, and from the coast of Tyre and Sidon, who had come to hear him and to be healed of their diseases. Those troubled by evil spirits were cured, and the people all tried to touch him, because power was coming from him and healing them all." (Luke 6:17-19) "After this, Jesus traveled about from one town and village to another, proclaiming the good news of the Kingdom of God. The Twelve were with him, and also some women who had been cured of evil spirits and diseases." (Luke 8:1-2)

What Percy wanted to make sure we all understood was that *we*, as believers, who walk in the power of the Holy Spirit, also have the authority to cast out demons and heal the sick. "When Jesus had called the Twelve together, he gave them power and authority to drive out all demons and to cure diseases, and he sent them out to preach the kingdom of God and to heal the sick." (Luke 9:1-2) We then see in Luke 10, "After this the Lord appointed seventy-two others and sent them two by two ahead of him to every town and place where he was about to go. He told them, 'The harvest is plentiful, but the workers are few. Ask the Lord of the harvest, therefore, to send out workers into his harvest field. Go! I am sending you out like lambs among wolves.' The seventy-two returned with joy and said, 'Lord, even the demons submit to us in your name.'"(Luke 10:1-3, 17)

Folks, *this* is what you and I are supposed to be doing. This is what Jesus intended for us when He went back to heaven and sent the Holy Spirit to be with us. "Not by might nor by power, but by my Spirit." (Zech. 4:6) Oh, that we would believe and begin to walk in the power the Lord has already given us when we received Him; that we would demonstrate that power in us as Scripture says. "My message and my preaching were not with wise and persuasive words, but with a demonstration of the Spirit's power, so that your faith might not rest on men's wisdom, but on God's power." (1 Cor. 2:4-5)

The response to Percy and Sara Jo's visit was so enthusiastic (that's good fruit), that I ended up inviting them back again. Percy and Sara Jo continue to minister inner healing and deliverance out of their home in Charlotte, and Percy lectures and ministers at churches and events around the city and state. They are Spiritual parents to many and a total blessing to our community.

Reunion Coffee

In August of 2009, I felt led to host a coffee to kick off the fall meetings. I ended up inviting all the women who at one time or another had come to my home for a prayer meeting. I felt it was a way to honor the Lord in all He had done. In hindsight, I think it was also a way to honor all the women who over the years took time out to come be with Him and sit at His feet. I also now see it was perhaps a type of closure as this six year season was coming to an end.

I did not know then that this season of gatherings was coming to a close; but the Lord knew. I am so glad we all had that opportunity to revisit with one another again as some women who came had not visited since 2004. It was a great time of reconnecting and sharing. The morning was designed to be a social time, a time to revisit, and a time to testify to what the Lord had done.

The Glory Girls continued to meet every other week and our routine revolved around Listening Prayer. On the home front, Rob and I were being presented with some shaking of our own. Rob's dad, Marion Cochran, aka "Granddaddy" was admitted into hospice the day before the reunion coffee. He had pulmonary fibrosis. The remainder of the year was spent praying for his last days and visiting him and Rob's mom in Greensboro. It was an emotional roller coaster as we found ourselves in uncharted territory. Both Rob's parents and mine were alive at this time in our lives. In April of 2010, Granddaddy died. But in the midst of his last months, God's peace that passes all understanding guarded our hearts. The real blessing was that Granddaddy knew where he was going. He knew Jesus and he knew he was going to heaven. I did not realize until after he was gone how precious a gift it is to know that your loved one knows Jesus and therefore has eternal life.

Reflection

Is there a shaking going on in your life? At work? In your marriage? Is there something going on with one of your children that is overwhelming and causing you concern and worry and stress? Maybe you have elderly parents and the new territory of taking care of them is causing some shaking, emotionally as well as physically. From where does your help come? I hope your help comes from God the Father, God the Son and God the Holy Spirit. The Word is one place to go to when the shaking is all around you. I pray as you learn to hear the voice of the Lord, the Spirit will direct you to Scripture. It is full of words of comfort, hope, security, and love. Deuteronomy 32:47 tells us that God's words are not just idle words, but they are life. Grab hold of the Word today and let it be an anchor for you in the midst of the shaking.

Prayer

Lord, today I decree that You are my rock. You are my anchor. You, Lord, are my strongtower. You know more about what is happening in my life than I even do. I confess to You today that the storm I am in is difficult. I am asking today, in Jesus' Name, for Your help. I give You permission to shake whatever needs to be shaken in order for right change to occur. Lord, I want to be in right alignment with You. Lord, I know that You can bring calm in the middle of the storm. I am asking for a supernatural release of Your peace and Your calm today. I also want to thank You for Your Word. It is an anchor. Show me passages that I can hold onto when the storms and the shaking are all around me. I trust You, knowing You love me and desire the best for me and my life. Lord, I need You. Come and be with me today. I ask this in Jesus' Name. Amen

Suggested Bible Reading

Meditate on Psalm 18 and claim the Lord as your support, your rock and your support.

CHAPTER 18

Winds of Change

WE ARE A TRIUNE PERSON just like God is. We are made up of a spirit, a soul, and a body. Our body is our flesh. Our soul is our mind, our will, our emotion, and our heart. And our spirit is God in us. On my fiftieth birthday, I was given a book titled *Blessing Your Spirit* by Sylvia Gunter and Arthur Burk. It is an amazing book full of blessings to be prayed over your spirit. 1 Thessalonians 5:23-24 says: "May God himself, the God of peace, sanctify you through and through. May your whole *spirit, soul and body* be kept blameless at the coming of our Lord Jesus Christ. The one who calls you is faithful and he will do it." (Emphasis added.)

The Word says "spirit, soul and body" in that passage from Thessalonians. It does not say body, soul, and spirit, which is the way people usually quote it. Spirit is mentioned first, and that is a clue to its importance. Our spirit is the handprint of God in us and our spirit is designed to be the head honcho over our soul and our body. In our Western culture, we tend to nurture and develop our bodies and our souls long before we ever think about nurturing or developing our spirit.

I was so taken by this book and the new revelations I was reading in it, I eventually ended up buying several copies to give away as I felt led by the Lord. Over time, many of the Glory Girls became interested in learning more about blessing the spirit, and consequently, we began to unpack this new truth together. As we became more familiar with blessing our own spirits, we began blessing one another's spirits. Connie May, who had been in Florida for two years because of her husband's job transfer, had also learned of Arthur Burk and the ministry of blessing your spirit. The women's group she became involved with while in Jacksonville was using *Blessing Your Spirit* too to minister to one another. When Connie moved back to Charlotte in 2009 and we made this connection, we all knew that this revelation we were getting was important. You can probably guess what happened next. I emailed Arthur to see if we could meet him.

Arthur Burk

Arthur Burk's ministry, Sapphire Leadership Group, is based out of Anaheim, California. Location had never stopped the Lord in the past from providing our group what we needed to grow in relationship with Him, so I figured if God wanted us to know more about blessing the spirit, and if He wanted us to understand some other things we were hearing about through Arthur's ministry, He would line it up for us to learn about these things.

When I emailed Arthur, I told him that his book, *Blessing Your Spirit* had been a real gift to us as a group, and if he ever found his way to Charlotte, we would love to meet him and host him. Sure enough, Arthur wrote back. Unbeknownst to us, Arthur has a satellite office in Spartanburg, South Carolina, less than two hours away. The next thing we knew, twelve Glory Girls were heading to Spartanburg early one Saturday morning in November to meet the man himself.

We spent the entire morning with Arthur, getting to know him as he shared deep spiritual revelation with us and some of his own personal testimony. It was fascinating. Arthur talked to us about blessing our spirit, he talked to us about the seven redemptive gifts we read about in Romans 12, and he touched on a third topic, land anointing and redeeming the land, which confirmed what Godfrey Birtill had talked to us about a year earlier. Arthur was expanding our horizons, broadening our tent pegs if you will, and we were intrigued.

After Arthur had been sharing with us for about two hours, he was ready to wrap up the morning. Yours truly asked if he would be willing to bless each one of our spirits before we left. Bold move, I know. What ended up happening was a total surprise. Arthur ended up blessing my spirit to show the group how to do it. The interesting part of it all was I also received some generational healing before the blessing began.

It all began with a picture the Holy Spirit gave Arthur. In this picture he saw a big house, and the Lord showed him that my spirit was living in only part of the house. He said it looked like I was restricting myself to live in the bedroom, the bathroom, and the kitchen only. Then Arthur said: "There's a bunch of house there that you don't sense the need for and you're not exploring, but the rest of the house is a treasure chest of resources. And I asked the Father why you are not exploring. He said that it was a generational issue, that the spirit of innovation and exploration has been roundly cursed in the past." Arthur, with my permission, began prayer ministry that involved deliverance from past generational bondage and curses. I had no problem being ministered to in front of everyone. I was getting the personal benefit of ministry, and everyone else was getting a close up look at another deliverance ministry style. I don't know that I can make sense of it all: the supernatural is not always easy to explain. The best I can say is that

I felt in the core of my being that something very old and restricting was being shaken loose so I could walk in a new level of wholeness and adventure.

After the prayer ministry, I had some time to be still while Arthur explained to the others what he had just prayed. Then, he looked me in the eyes and began to bless my spirit. One of the key sentences Arthur said to me was this: "Today is the beginning of a whole new chapter for you." I later wrote in my journal: "New beginning. Hallmark day. 11/14/2009." I did not know what this new chapter would look like but I knew it was true.

I think I can speak for all of us and say that when we left Spartanburg that day, our heads were spinning but our spirits were soaring. We instinctively knew that Arthur was providing a deep well of revelation we had not yet tapped into. The Lord was taking us on another expedition to discover new, undiscovered truth. We left with excitement and zeal to pursue this new revelation. We all believed God was presenting another opportunity to us to grow deeper in our knowledge of Him.

As a group, we immediately began putting the spirit blessing into practice. We also began to look into the redemptive gift teaching. Libby has a powerful testimony as a result of her spirit being blessed, and Connie has come into deep understanding about redemptive gifts. Here, in their own words, is some of what we have learned and experienced as we have pursued this new revelation, and applied it to our lives.

"Blessing Your Spirit," by Libby Walker

I have lived most of my life with a sense of knowing that I had eight cylinders, but was only running on two. From early childhood, my life was disrupted with illness, including chronic depression and colitis. I then lost a brother to cancer, had family relationship challenges, and marriage that ended in divorce. I am also a mother of a child with genetic anomaly and severe autism. Then in 1994, I was diagnosed with lupus. As a result, I was put on disability and lost my career as a clinical nurse specialist in women's health. For the last seventeen years, my weekly regimen consists of doctor appointments, lab work, IV treatments, and physical therapy.

Because of the amount of trauma that had been part of my life, I was able to function, but not really live. I was going through the motions of life without being able to really connect. I tried everything I knew to do to improve this situation, holding onto hope that life could and should be better. Consequently, I spent year after year praying for wholeness, and I pursued many avenues of counseling and prayer ministry for physical and inner healing.

For my birthday in 2009, Anne gave me a book titled *Blessing Your Spirit* by Sylvia Gunter and Arthur Burk. I sensed it was no ordinary book and immediately began reading it.

Two revelations I read about in the book really caught my attention. First was the revelation that the spirit can be broken. I was familiar with the Scripture from Proverbs 13:12 that says: "Hope deferred makes the heart sick." In my journey, I had given much thought to the continued disappointments and heartbreaks that had been so difficult for me to endure. I had grown very weary, and I was certain my heart was sick. I passionately wanted my heart to be healed.

The second thing I began to understand is that we are called by the Father to accomplish His unique purposes for our life *and* for His kingdom. We are to be about His work. Brokenness and wounding within can thwart our purposes. In this book, I learned that by blessing our spirit, by calling it forward to reign over our soul and our physical body, a supernatural healing can take place. And I later found that this healing can happen so much sooner than going through hours of therapy and prayer.

I remember thinking about the Scripture in Ecclesiastes 1:9 that says, "there is nothing new under the sun." Even though this idea of blessing your spirit sounded new to me, I knew I was reading deep revelation, and I was excited about it and wanted to experience it.

As this revelation continued to unfold for me personally and for our prayer group, the Glory Girls began to practice blessing one another's spirits at our meetings.

September 2, 2009 became a pivotal day in my life. At the end of our meeting, Connie May began ministering to me by blessing my spirit as she was learning to do through Sylvia and Arthur's book. She invited the Holy Spirit to come, and then began to listen to what the Lord would have her say to bless my spirit. I don't know that I can explain it but I felt a powerful shift occur in my soul and in my body. I was overwhelmed by the love I was feeling as she prayed, and it brought me to tears.

In the days that followed, it became obvious to me and to others that something had changed. People began to comment that my appearance was changing, especially the nurses I had seen regularly over the years for lupus. One of the nurses said, "I had to look twice to see if it was you." Another one commented, "You have such a bright smile. You are radiant." Still another nurse said, "Your face looks different. Your color is different. Before, you looked so pale and fragile. I usually thought you were going to faint when I had to draw your blood."

But one of the most astounding comments came from a registered nurse that has administered IV treatments to me for years. One day soon after the blessing of my spirit, I went in for one of my IV treatments, and when I sat down, Nurse Peggy said, "I don't recognize this arm! Here is a vein popping up ready to go and usually I have to search for one. What have you been doing?" The words "vein popping up" were an indication to me that my physical health had increased and my body was showing signs of that truth. I *knew* these outward changes were a direct result of the prayers I had received blessing my spirit.

I began to feel a stronger, purer sense of identity, and I felt less paralyzed by the circumstances of my past. It felt like I was coming to life in a way I have never known before. I continued to receive prayers to bless my spirit, and I began to feel a new sense of joy and the beginning of an integration of parts that had been at war.

I am growing increasingly stronger each day, and increasingly more excited about life. Hope that is always present for each one of us has now come alive for me. I appreciate the gift of life and look forward to fulfilling my destiny. I am beginning to walk in a freedom that I have never known since my spirit has been blessed. I am not sure how it all works. It is a supernatural process. But this has been my experience and I am profoundly grateful.

(Libby is an original Glory Girl. We call her Liberty, as she continues to be a sign and a wonder of God's hope, provision, and healing grace.)

"What the Redemptive Gifts Revelation Has Meant to Me," by Connie May

"Christianity is designed to work!" This was a phrase that captured my attention and inspired me to seriously study the Redemptive Gifts teaching by Arthur Burk. Spiritual gifts are first mentioned in Romans 12, and I had heard numerous sermons and teachings on spiritual gifts, and had even taken many tests to discover more about what the Scriptures say about how Christ in you is supposed to work. However, everything I studied proved to be minimally helpful.

Romans 12:6-8 says: "We have different gifts, according to the grace given us. If a man's gift is *prophesying*, let him use it in proportion to his faith. If it is *serving*, let him serve; if it is *teaching*, let him teach; if it is *encouraging*, let him encourage; if it is *contributing to the needs of others*, let him give generously; if it is *leadership*, let him govern diligently; if it is *showing mercy*, let him do it cheerfully." (Emphasis added.)

As we grow in the Christian walk, we are to develop in all seven redemptive gifts and we are also supposed to have all of the fruits of the Spirit. Somehow, that reality seemed a long way off from my reality. So, I was intrigued.

Like many of you, my childhood was loving and safe. I was

taught that God is love and I experienced His love in family and community. I became aware of my need for a Savior before my twelfth birthday. I experienced the baptism of the Holy Spirit at age seventeen. I was in a denominational church and there was very little language to express and understand that experience, but it was a loving community that was caring and supportive.

My experiences changed as I grew and went to college. I began to experience parts of life that were more difficult. This included illness and death, and what I refer to as, "times when the unimaginable happens." I experienced broken relationships and a Christianity that seemed to not work. In the brokenness, I accepted that life had pain and I understood death was a part of life.

I became a nurse and I also worked with the youth in our church and community. I enjoyed relationships, but often worked on church and community committees that were functioning way below what I read in Scripture. I married, had a family, and I continued to need more of God in my life. I studied the Bible more deliberately through many wonderful teachers, including five years in Bible Study Fellowship. I continually searched for more truth to apply to my life and my family's life. After having been on this Christian journey for forty-three years, I was introduced to the Redemptive Gifts teaching and Arthur Burk.

The study of the redemptive gifts is a collaboration of study over the past several decades "by the body of Christ for the body of Christ," according to Arthur Burk. He and many men and women have studied the work of Bill Gothard, John Sandford, and many others who longed to see Christianity work. They have provided us with a wealth of information that works in real life. The redemptive gift study is built upon their lifetimes of study and is still being unlocked by the body of Christ today. It has helped me view my life and experiences from heaven's side in order to reframe my perspective. I now see my life as the playing field I was born into that would allow me to accomplish my purpose. The good and the other experiences of life have redemptive purposes.

In this study, the focus is on God's design of creation and humanity. The earth and the scientific laws that govern principles for life on this planet, including spiritual, natural, physical, and chemical laws, laws of science and physics, are all designed to work. God didn't design life to be broken. Jesus didn't give His life so we could remain broken! Jesus said, "I came that they may have life and have it to the full." (John 10:10)

As I studied our design, using the seven redemptive gifts study, I began to see how God designed me, my husband, our children, my parents, our brothers and sisters and so on. I began to understand why there are fractured relationships. I am not referring to sin, but to a lack of fulfillment and joy in relationships. Using a kitchen analogy: It is like using a spoon when you need a knife to cut an apple, and becoming frustrated because the stupid thing doesn't work. A spoon was not designed to cut an apple. In the same way, someone designed to be an administrator is not the best person to serve others. Rather, they are designed to lead, build and create effective systems and teams. Or the person who is designed to be artistic and sensitive to the Holy Spirit is great at leading worship, but they may not be the best one to work in a nursery with crying children.

The redemptive gifts are our "hard wiring from God."[19] Each and every person is created by God as a one of a kind masterpiece, created to solve problems and enjoy life on this planet, before going to Heaven. The Bible tells us we are the crown of his creation. Psalm 8:5-6 says: "When I look at your heavens, the work of your fingers, the moon and stars that you set in place-what are mere mortals, that you concern yourself with them; humans, that you watch over them with such care? You made him a little lower than the angels, you crowned him with glory and honor, you had him rule what your hands made, you put everything under his feet." (CJB) There is something very special about each individual, and we are all needed to bring our unique gifting into the fullness of our design so that we accomplish our purpose and potential.

Now, for those of you who are beginning to think those dreadful thoughts: "Why am I hearing this now? I am too old," let me remind you Moses, Joshua and Caleb did not do their most significant work until they were in their eighties. And remember Abraham and Sarah? God does not view things the ways we do. So dismiss that thought, or it will lead you into regret and you will miss what God is doing today.

Mark 12:30-31 says, "'Love the Lord your God with all your heart and with all your soul and with all your mind and with all your strength.' The second is this: 'Love your neighbor as yourself.' There is no commandment greater than these." To be in proper relationship with Father God, and with those in our community, we need to keep the first commandment first. Then we will propel the body of Christ in the earth to be a living, functioning force. Understanding the master plan simplifies and accelerates fruitfulness in our lives. This does not mean that it is simple or easy, but hard work has never been more rewarding or fulfilling than this.

Understanding our purposes in the kingdom, our relationships, our battlefields, our strengths, and weakness are a huge benefit to us and to those in our community. Jesus, our Redeemer, has a plan where He will be "making everything new." (Rev. 21:5) In the Revelation of Jesus Christ, John writes, "And I heard a loud voice from the throne saying, 'Now the dwelling of God is with men, and he will live with them. They will be his people, and God himself will be with them and be their God. He will wipe every tear from their eyes. There will be no more death or mourning or crying or pain, for the old order of things has passed away.' He who was seated on the throne said, 'I am making everything new.' Then he said, 'Write this down, for these words are trustworthy and true.' He said to me, 'It is done. I am the Alpha and the Omega, the Beginning and the End. To him who is thirsty I will give to drink without cost from the spring of the water of life. He who overcomes will inherit all this, and I will be his God and he will be my son.'" (Rev. 21:3-7)

The redemptive gifts teaching is a tool you can use to discover your design, and when you have a restored relationship with your Heavenly Father through Jesus Christ, these teachings will help know your birthright, your battlefield, and how the enemy has successfully stolen things and relationships from you that the Father had always intended for you to have. Charles Wale has put this material in a workbook called, "Designed for Fulfillment, A Study of the Redemptive Gifts." It's like a road map to help you unlock your potential.

As you develop character, you will walk in more and more authority to accomplish your God-given assignment. And you will enjoy more and more freedom and life as Jesus described it. Jesus is the perfect example of a human walking in the fullness of His birthright. Scripture says He is the firstborn of many sons. Walking in sonship is the goal of all believers who walk in their identity in Christ Jesus.

Jesus did what we could not do. He lived his life perfectly, sinless. Then, He trusted the Father with the rest. The great exchange! Jesus is the Redeemer. He is the one who takes the part of life that has been less than what the Father intended, and He has a redemptive plan already prepared to take away the bitterness, the pain, the loss, the grief, the heart ache we have become intimately acquainted with. He exchanges it with what Jesus knew: intimate joy with His heavenly Father.

(Connie is an original Glory Girl. She has been a mentor and teacher to the group and continues to help us mature in the revelation of the Holy Spirit.)

As you can see, this new revelation we were receiving was becoming life-altering. Libby and Connie are sharing just two of many, many testimonies of how the lives of the Glory Girls have been changed though blessing our spirits and understanding our redemptive gifts. Meeting Arthur was quite a way to end not only 2009, but also our six years together as a group. The Lord was once again going to shift things for us, but He made sure He had the necessary things in place to help us move on to our next destination on the Kingdom road.

Reflection

The information presented here may be new revelation to you. It was new to us as a group, but profound in its truth. *Blessing Your Spirit* by Sylvia Gunter and Arthur Burk and *Designed for Fulfillment, A Study of the Redemptive Gifts* by Charles R. Wale Jr. are both important tools to have in your spiritual tool belt. I want to suggest you prayerfully consider tapping into one or both of these resources.

It's time we all walked in our full potential. It is time for your spirit to be recognized and legitimized and it is time you had a clearer understanding of how you were made through the redemptive gift study. These teachings are critical for us as believers to begin understanding as we walk in our destiny call. So if you are ready to dig deeper into God's revelatory truths, go for it. Wonderful treasures are there just waiting to be uncovered. And as you wade into deeper waters, I pray the eyes of your heart and your mind will be opened to receive all it is the Lord has for you through these two studies.

Below is a prayer you can pray today to bless your spirit. It is just an example of what blessing your spirit can look like. Get quiet and read this blessing over yourself. I pray that your spirit be awakened today in Jesus' Name.

Blessing Your Spirit Prayer

Today, I call my human spirit forward in the Name of Jesus. Although my soul and body are also precious in the sight of the Lord, I ask my soul and my body to step aside for just a minute so my spirit can be blessed.

Spirit, I want to bless you this day by declaring truth over you. You are fearfully and wonderfully made. You are the handprint of God in me. You are unique. You are special. You have a purpose and I need you to be fully active in my life. Today I give you permission to begin taking the lead in guiding my soul and my body so that I can be about God's kingdom purposes here on earth. You have a special set of treasures deposited in you, and I pray, beginning today, that those treasures you carry will be released in my life in Jesus' Name.

I speak to you, spirit, and bless you in order to recognize you, legitimize you, and acknowledge you. I bless your destiny path. May you, in conjunction with the Holy Spirit, lead me in my God-ordained walk. I bless you to release new hope, new vision, new peace, new anticipation, and new discovery in my life. And I bless you spirit to be a blessing to others.

I invite you now to look into the Father's face and tune your ears to His voice so that the light from heaven can shine in my life and reveal truth. I bless you to reveal to me what the Father is doing so I can be aligned with Him. Today is the day of new beginnings. As you begin taking your God-ordained place in my life, I bless this first step to begin this new walk and new way of life. Thank you spirit for all that you are in me. I bless you this day, in Jesus' Name. Amen

Suggested Bible Readings

Psalm 139

Other Books

Prayer Portions by Sylvia Gunter
Living In His Presence by Sylvia Gunter
Alive with Passion and Purpose by Sandy Landry

CHAPTER 19

It's a Wrap–Sabbath Rest

A WHOLE NEW WORLD OF deep Spiritual revelation had been presented to us. In true form, we bought many books and CDs while in Spartanburg to bring home with us so we could begin to delve into these new Spiritual truths Arthur had talked to us about. We were excited about the challenge and the opportunity to grow in deeper in our design and calling. I think all twelve of us left Spartanburg that day with a new sense of purpose, and an understanding that the Lord was introducing us to Arthur for a reason. When we seek the Lord's ways above all else, He meets us and takes us further still. We knew it was transition time again, and were ready to embrace whatever it looked like.

The winds of change were upon us, and I knew it was the Lord bringing the change. One December email devotion said: "New territory is before you. You have not walked where you are about to walk. There is no map except the one I have programmed in you. Your inner life is about to be enhanced to become like a GPS that never fails. You have flown by sight thus far but now you begin instrumentation and learning to trust *My* GPS." Another said, "Dig new wells." No doubt about it, the Glory Girls were digging new wells, and we were traveling into new territory.

The Lord also gave me a personal word: "The winds of change are coming. They will blow you in a new direction. Do not fret. Keep your face tilted towards Mine. New opportunities. New weapons of warfare. New hopes. New visions. New horizons. As the rain comes, so will My winds—though they bring change, even destruction, you will move out in greater force, greater unction, greater power manifesting Me. Hold on. Hold onto Me. My hand. It is there. Grab hold and watch. A new day dawning."

On December 29, 2009, the Scripture verse from 1 Corinthians 2:9 came across in an email devotion and it said: "No eye has seen, no ear has heard, no mind has conceived what God has prepared for those who love him." God was calling us to trust Him as He invited us to move with His Spirit. And with reverent awe, we answered, "Yes and Amen, Lord, Yes and Amen."

On January 4, 2010, I was scheduled for Jury Duty. I packed my bag full of teaching CDs, and I packed a book Arthur had recommended by Alistair Petrie titled *Releasing Heaven on Earth.* Ever since my ministry with Arthur, I had declared that I wanted to begin to explore the "unexplored" rooms of my house. That word and the picture Arthur had shared with me had made such sense to me. I've always known there was more out there for me to explore and discover, and I wanted to venture out into the "other rooms," although I had no idea what that looked like or how to even begin.

As the day went on, I eventually pulled out Alistair's book. When I opened it up, I could not believe what was staring me in the face. There in front of me was the following Scripture from Exodus 23:10-13: "For six years you are to sow your fields and harvest the crops, but during the seventh year let the land lie unplowed and unused. Then the poor among your people may get food from it, and the wild animals may eat what they leave. Do the same with your vineyard and your olive grove. Six days do your work, but on the seventh day do not work, so that your ox and your donkey may rest and the slave born in your household, and the alien as well, may be refreshed. *Be careful to do everything I have said to you.*" (Emphasis added.)

I just sat there, completely still. All I can tell you is that when I read those words, a Holy fear came over me like nothing I had ever experienced. I knew right then and there that the Lord was calling me to a Sabbath rest from hosting meetings. This was not the first time that Scripture had popped out in front of me in recent months, but it was the first time I experienced such a trembling towards them. I knew I had to obey.

I had been hosting home meetings since January 2004. The past six years had been amazing. But the time had now come to take a rest and I was getting a clear directive. When I got home that evening from Jury Duty, I sat right down at the computer and drafted a letter to the Glory Girls, telling them what had happened. I then told them that I was going to have to rely on someone else to host the meetings in 2010. I had made the decision to follow the word I was getting, and honor the Lord with obedience. I got immediate confirmation from most all of the girls who believed this was right. Many later said they could see it coming.

This decision was not as easy as it may sound here. As I have said earlier, there is a real sense of security in the daily, weekly, monthly commitments we get involved in. Fear of the unknown can trap us into staying where we are. We can also put our identity in what we are doing and therefore, the fear of leaving a position, whether in a church environment or a work situation, can deter the Lord's next step for us. But Scripture tells us He is patient. The Lord will wait until we are ready to move again. I do wonder, though, how much time we lose on our destiny path when we stay stuck in something and don't obey His direction to move out.

The Glory Girls had grown to love and depend on one another.

Our time together was like drinking life-giving water from a well. But we also had grown up enough to know we had to be willing to trust. And we were seeing that the Lord had already gone before us with provisions that would sustain us. Arthur had already put in place plans to begin hosting meetings once a month in Spartanburg starting in January 2010. So, on the second Saturday of every month, many of the Glory Girls would caravan to South Carolina for a morning of teaching. The Lord was hosting our meetings in a new and unique way, and we became connected with other men and women of faith who were on this Great Adventure with us.

Connie May offered to host the meetings in her home for the year, and as the Spirit has led, the meetings continued. Several of the women went back to work. Some got involved with Bible studies in the community, and a couple of the women began volunteering at the county jail. When we wouldn't see each other for a couple of weeks, one of the women would send out an email with a lunch day and time, and we would meet for lunch. We have done just as much intercession in local restaurants around the city during those lunches as we did in all our home meetings. Interesting isn't it. Who would have thought that our time together could look like that?

The summer came and went, and the fall fast approached. When I met two girlfriends for lunch in August 2010, and they asked when I was going to start writing my book, I had no idea I would be finishing the first draft of this book by Thanksgiving. The time was right. The prophecy spoken years earlier in 2003 about a book was now ready to be acted upon. All I had to do was take the little mustard seed off the shelf and begin planting it.

So here we are. It is 2011 and I am now looking into publishing options after rounds of editing with Betsy Thorpe. There are decisions to make about how to share this book with others. I am trusting the Lord in that decision too.

My Christian walk has taught me that the Lord, Creator of the universe, has a deep yearning to have a relationship with each one of us. We are His children. He hopes more than anything that we will invite Him in to our lives and sup with Him and talk to Him and share all our fears and dreams, our hopes and concerns, our desires and our vision with Him. He desires that not one will be left behind or forgotten. It is hard to put into words how grateful I am that I have come into relationship with Father God, Jesus Christ, and the Holy Spirit. Grateful really does not even touch the true meaning of how thankful I am and how marvelous my life has been as a result of saying "Yes" to Jesus! My prayer is that everyone who reads this story will take the first step and invite Jesus into their heart. He is waiting. And then, invite the Holy Spirit to be fully released in your life. I believe He will not only hear your prayer, but He will answer it.

Reflection / Conclusion

I hope that by sharing this story, your heart has grown in a better understanding of who the Lord is. I hope that a new desire has been unleashed in you, a new desire to pursue God to get to know Him better. I hope that today marks a new beginning for you to begin or further your relationship with God the Father, Jesus His Son, and the Wonderful Counselor, the Holy Spirit.

The Holy Spirit is an amazing person. He can be quiet and serene, and He can be the wildest partier around. His ways are higher and deeper and wider than anything we can possible imagine with our mind. He is like the wind: invisible, surprising, ever-present, and real. Life in the Spirit at times can even look messy. But isn't life messy at times? The Holy Spirit can really shake things up. He will challenge our intellect. He will challenge our senses. He will challenge our common sense. He can move us out of our comfort zone. This is the reality of the life of the Holy Spirit. But don't let fear rob you of the immense joy and fun and supernatural life the Holy Spirit has to share. Jesus would not have left this earth and sent the Holy Spirit to us if we did not need Him in our lives.

Jesus said, "If you love me, you will obey what I command. And

I will ask the Father, and he will give you another Counselor to be with you forever—The Spirit of truth. The world cannot accept him, because it neither sees him nor knows him. But you know him, for he lives with you and will be in you." (John 14:15-17)

Get still before the Lord, and ask Him where to begin. I believe the Holy Spirit will speak clearly to you. One thing you may want to do is get yourself a good Study Bible. There are many to choose from and any of the Christian Book stores can direct you. You may also want to touch base with some friends and begin meeting in someone's home. Or maybe you want to join a Bible Study group. This journey is not to be walked alone. We need one another to grow. Don't be a lone ranger. I have seen firsthand the ill-effects of those who chose to do it their way without support, encouragement, and correction from the Body. I also will pray that if there is a particular book for you to tap into or a ministry site for you to explore, the Holy Spirit will give you clear direction. In the back of this book is a list of all the different books and ministries I have mentioned. My prayer is that you will take advantage of them. I know that I have only shared a fraction of what is out there, but I do believe you are at a good starting place.

All you have to do is take the first step. The Lord will meet you and lead you on. It's time to begin to walk in your destiny call. It's all about Him anyway! Come on. Open your hand. The Lord is offering you a mustard seed today. I hope you will receive it and begin the greatest adventure of all.

My Prayer for You

I pray that the Father will arrest your heart today. I pray that you will know to the core of your being that Jesus is the One who connects you with Father God, the Creator of the universe. Jesus said, "I am the way and the truth and the life. No one comes to the Father except through me." (John 14:6) We experience real life when we accept Jesus as our Lord and Savior. This is either fact or fiction. It can't be both, and it can't be partially correct. I have come to know it as fact. My relationship with the Father God, Jesus Christ, and the Holy Spirit these last twenty years confirms this truth for me.

"Come to the free living and drink of it as often as you like." Those words were not just for me. They are an invitation for you too. Come. Give your life to Jesus. Invite the Holy Spirit to be fully released in your life. Be born again into new life. "I keep asking that the God of our Lord Jesus Christ, the glorious Father, may give you the Spirit of wisdom and revelation, so that you may know him better. I pray also that the eyes of your heart may be enlightened in order that you may know the hope to which he has called you, the riches of his glorious inheritance in the saints, and his incomparably great power for us who believe. That power is like the working of his mighty strength, which he exerted in Christ when he raised him from the dead and seated him at his right hand in the heavenly realms, far above all rule and authority, power and dominion, and every title that can be given, not only in the present age but also in the one to come. And God placed all things under his feet and appointed him to be head over everything for the church, which is his body, the fullness of him who fills everything in every way." (Eph. 1:17-23) "I pray that out of his glorious riches he may strengthen you with power through his Spirit in your inner being, so that Christ may dwell in your hearts through faith. And I pray that you, being rooted and established in love, may have power, together with all the saints, to grasp how wide and long and high and deep is the love of Christ, and to know this love that surpasses knowledge—that you may be filled to the measure of all the fullness of God. Now to him who is able to do immeasurably more than all we ask or imagine, according to his power that is at work within us, *to him be glory in the church and in Christ Jesus throughout all generations, for ever and ever! Amen.*" (Eph. 3:16-21) (Emphasis added.)

Blessings to you through Him who saves. Blessings to you, this day, in Jesus' Name. Amen

NOTES

Chapter 3: New Life in The Spirit

1. Shekinhah: *www.bible-history.com/tabernacle/TAB4The_Shekinah_Glory.htm*

Chapter 6: Moving On and Moving Out

2. Epiphany: Definition from *Webster's New Collegiate Dictionary* © 1976 by G. & C. Merriam Co.

Chapter 8: The Outpouring Part 1

3. Personal information about John Scotland found on www.johnscotland.org.

Chapter 9: The Outpouring Part 2

4. "The Wine of the Kingdom (One Shall Tell Another). Words and Music by Graham Kendrick. © 1981 Kingsway Thankyou Music

5. Personal information about Alan Smith found on www. stoneypointpublishing.com.

Chapter 10: The Outpouring Part 3

6. Personal Information about Kimber Britner written by Kimber Britner. For more information about Kimber and her ministry, go to: www.moxieme.com.

7. Information from the website for John and Paula Sandford with the Elijah House School of Ministry: www.elijahhouse.org.

8. Poem "Hope" by Anne Cochran inspired by the Holy Spirit June 17, 2005.

Chapter 11: The Elijah House School of Ministry

9. Used with permission from Elijah House Ministries from *School of Prayer Ministry—Basic One*. Page 35.

Chapter 13: On Our Own

10. "Take My Life," by Scott Underwood ⊠1995 Mercy/Vineyard Publishing (Administered by Music Services Inc.)

11. "Turn Your Eyes Upon Jesus." Words: Helen H, Lemmel 1922; Music: Helen H Lemmel, 1922.

Chapter 14: Listening Prayer

12. "Captivate Us Lord Jesus." A word from the Lord at our Glory Girl Meeting on March 4, 2007.

Chapter 15: A Step Out In Faith

13. Refrain from the Hymn, "Trust and Obey." Words: John H. Sammis, 1887; Music: Daniel B. Towner, 1887.

14. Personal information about Godfrey Birtill found on www. godfreyb.com.

15. Line from the song, "Lift Up Your Heads (Alleluia)."

16. "Lift Up Your Heads (Alleluia)" by James Montgomery 1771-1854 (Moravian Hymn Book).

Godfrey Birtill (music) and Adaptation, © 2003 Thankyou Music UK.

17: "I Will Stand" Godfrey Birtill © 2003 Thankyou Music UK.

Chapter 16: The Calm in the Storm

18. "Spirit Song." Words: John Wimber, 1979. Music: John Wimber, 1979. 1979 © Mercy Publishing.

Chapter 18: Winds of Change

19. Term "hard wiring from God" from *Redemptive Gift Workbook* © 2007 Charles R. Wale Jr. For more information, go to www.freetobeministries.com.

REFERENCES

Chapter 1: Let The Great Adventure Begin

Conversation With God: Experiencing the Life-Changing Impact of Personal Prayer by Lloyd John Ogilvie (www.amazon.com)

Chapter 2: Double Blessing

Blue Water by Sheila Walsh (www.sheilawalsh.com)

The Sword of the Spirit; The Word of God by Joy Lamb (www.theswordofthespiritbook.com)

Experiencing The Spirit by Robert Heidler (www.gloryofzion.org)

The Gifts of the Spirit by Derek Prince (www.derekprince.org)

Chapter 3: New Life in The Spirit

Nine O'Clock in the Morning by Dennis and Rita Bennett (www.amazon.com)

The Holy Spirit and You by Dennis Bennett (www.amazon.com)

Dialogue With God by Mark Virkler (www.cwgministries.org)

Understanding the Dreams You Dream Volume 1 by Ira Milligan (www.servant-ministries.org)

From Generation to Generation: A Manual for Healing by Patricia A. Smith (www.amazon.com)

Miracle In Darien by Bob Slosser (www.amazon.com)

Intercessory Prayer by Dutch Sheets (www.dutchsheets.org)

Growing in the Prophetic by Mike Bickle (www.mikebickle.org)

To learn more about John Paul Jackson go to www.streammin-istries.com.

Chapter 4: Inner Healing, Soaking Prayer, and the Gift of Prophecy

The Beginner's Guide to the Gift of Prophecy by Jack Deere (www.jackdeere.com)

To learn more about MorningStar Publications and Ministries, go to www.morningstarministries.org.

To learn more about Chavda Ministries International, go to www.chavadaministries.org.

Chapter 5: Change Is Coming

Boundaires by Henry Cloud and John Townsend (www.cloud-townsend.com)

To learn more about Steve Shultz's The Elijah List, go to www.elijahlist.com.

To learn more about Joni James and ACTS Ministry (Activating Christians to Serve), go to www.joniames.com.

Chapter 8: The Outpouring Part 1

Strong's Concordance by James Strong (www.nelsonreference.com)

The Azusa Street Revival by Roberts Liardon (www.destinyimage.com)

Experiencing The Spirit by Robert Heidler (www.gloryofzion.org)

They Speak In Other Tongues by John L. Sherrill (www.Amazon.com)

Acts of the Holy Spirit; God's Power For Living by Lloyd J. Ogilvie (www.drlloydjohnogilvie.com)

To learn more about Anjie Carpenter, her ministry, and her music, go to www.anjiecarpenter.com.

To learn more about John Scotland and his ministry, go to www.johnscotland.org.

Chapter 9: The Outpouring Part 2

To learn more about Latha Ramesh Pandian and her ministry in Kuwait, go to www.vineyardministries.net.

Chapter 10: The Outpouring Part 3

To view Melissa Tyson Upham's jewelry, visit her website: www.glorytogoddesigns.com

To learn more about Kimber Britner and receive her free gifts, go to www.moxieme.com.

Chapter 11: The Elijah House School of Ministry

The Transformation of the Inner Man by John and Paula Sandford

Healing The Wounded Spirit by John and Paul Sandford

Restoring The Christian Family by John and Paula Sandford

The Renewal of the Mind by John L. Sanford and R. Loren Sandford.

Above four books can be found at www.elijahhouse.org.

Interpreting The Symbols and Types by Kevin J. Conner (www. CityBiblePublishing.com)

Understanding the Dreams you Dream Volume 2 by Ira Milligan (www.servant-ministries.org)

Chapter 12: The Train is Switching Tracks

Al Hardy is the Pastor of City Church Charlotte. To learn more about this church and their ministry, go to www.citychurchcharlotte.com.

Go to anjie@carolina.rr.com to subscribe to Anjie Carpenter's newsletter sharing truths about intimacy.

Chapter 13: On Our Own

*Joy In My Heart (www.childbiblesongs.com/song-04-ive-got-the-*joy-in-my-heart.*shtml)*

Chapter 14: Listening Prayer

The Voice of God by Cindy Jacobs (www.generals.org)

Chapter 15: A Step Out In Faith

To learn more about Godfrey Birtill, his ministry, and his music, go to www.godfreyb.com.

Chapter 17: Walking In Our Authority

The Prophets Notebook by Barry Kissell

Steve Shultz—The Elijah List (www.elijahlist.com)

To learn more about Ras and Bev Robinson, their testimony, their ministry, "What The Lord is Saying Today," and to subscribe to receive the daily prophetic words they publish online, go to www.fullnessonline.org.

To learn more about Derek Prince's ministry, go to www.derekprince.org.

Chapter 18: Winds of Change

Blessing Your Spirit by Sylvia Gunter and Arthur Burk (www.theslg.com)

Designed For Fulfillment, A Study for the Redemptive Gifts by Charles R. Wale (www.freetobeministries.com)

Prayer Portions by Sylvia Gunter (www.thefathersbusiness.com)

Living in His presence by Sylvia Gunter (www.thefathersbusiness.com)

Alive with Passion and Purpose by Sandy Landry (www.theslg.com)

To learn more about Sylvia Gunter and her ministry, The Father's Business, go to www.thefathersbusiness.com.

To learn more about Arthur Burk and his ministry, Sapphire Leadership Group, Inc, go to www.theslg.com.

Chapter 19: It's A Wrap—Sabbath Rest

Releasing Heaven on Earth by Alistair Petrie (www.arsenalbooks.com)

OTHER RESOURCES

I would be remiss if I did not mention four other people and their ministries that have had a profound impact on my life and the lives of the Glory Girls as we have learned about life in the Spirit. We have had an opportunity to meet several of them as they have visited Charlotte as guest speakers at conferences. Each one, in their own right, has a solid voice in training and equipping the Body to walk with the Holy Spirit, and each one is counted as a Spiritual parent to me.

1. Bill Johnson—Bethel Church (www.ibethel.com)
2. Patricia King—Extreme Prophetic (www.csa-xp.com)
3. Chuck Pierce—Glory Of Zion Church (www.gloryofzion.org)
4. Ryan Wyatt—Abiding Glory Church and International Ministry Base (www.abidingglory.com)

MUSIC

A few of my favorite Contemporary Christians artists are as follows.

Godfrey Birtill
Amber Brooks
Steven Curtis Chapman
Bethel Church (awesome worship CDs)
Elevation Church
I-HOP Worship Music (International House of Prayer, Kansas City, Kansas)
Third Day
Misty Edwards
Kelanie Glockler
Tim Hughes
Matt Maher
Julie Meyer
Chris Rice
Matt Redman
Alberto and Kimberly Rivera (Soaking Prayer music)
Michael W. Smith
Rita Springer
Chris Tomlin
Shelia Walsh

"The Spirit and the bride say, 'Come!' And let him who hears say, 'Come!' Whoever is thirsty, let him come; and whoever wishes, let him take the free gift of the water of life." **(Revelation 22:17)**

CPSIA information can be obtained at www.ICGtesting.com
Printed in the USA
BVOW072131240112

281312BV00001B/4/P